MOUNTAIN WALKING IN
AUSTRIA

Admonter Hut from Admonter Warte (Ennstaler Alps Walk 2)

MOUNTAIN WALKING IN
AUSTRIA

by
Cecil Davies

**A Guide to 25 Mountain Groups in the Eastern Alps
with 98 walks fully described**

Sketch maps and photographs by the author

CICERONE PRESS
MILNTHORPE, CUMBRIA

© Cecil Davies 1986
First published 1986
Reprinted 1988
New edition 1997
ISBN 1 85284 239 3
A catalogue record for this book is available from the British Library.

To MARIAN
my constant companion on these walks and to all who share our love

'for the chief things of the ancient mountains, and for
the precious things of the lasting hills.'

Front cover: Ellmauer Tor, Kaisergebirge, Group V

CONTENTS

THE MOUNTAIN GROUPS COVERED IN THE GUIDE

Boundaries of Mountain Groups in this guide.

National Boundaries

XII Number of Section in this guide

(15) Number of Group in the Alpenverein

Climbing N. Ridge, Hoher Freschen. (Bregenzerwaldgebirge Walk 1)

INTRODUCTION

Austria is the ideal country for the mountain walker.

The German and Austrian Alpine Clubs have over 500 mountain huts in Austria, linked by an incomparable system of hundreds of miles of footpaths. There are as many more mountain huts run by other clubs or privately. There are hundreds of summits of 2000m and over, and many over 3000m, which can be reached by walkers, many by simple walking and others by easy scrambling or on easy snow. Suitably equipped parties of three or more can extend their walking to include glaciers. A few such routes are included in this book, but the vast majority of these walks can be undertaken by anyone competent to walk on British hills. The scrambling which is met with on some walks is not harder than Crib Coch with its pinnacles or the North Ridge of Tryfan.

This is not a comprehensive guide to Austrian mountain walks: such a work would fill many volumes. It is an introduction to 25 mountain groups, with detailed descriptions of 98 walks varying in length from half a day to a good week. Using this guide as a starting point, you could soon work out additional walks in each group.

A feature of this book is that every walk described in detail has been personally walked by the author at least once between 1964 and 1995. Variations and additions not personally explored are bracketed and in smaller type. The 'lasting hills' do change: rockfall, avalanches, paths neglected or re-made, the retreat or advance of glaciation; all alter the character and difficulty of walks. Therefore each walk in this book is dated, so that users may judge for themselves whether to expect much change.

All information on huts, however, has been brought up-to-date from the Alpine Club's Green Hut Book, 1994.

Standards

Most of the walks are ungraded, which means that no rock-climbing at all is involved. Nevertheless, 'protected' routes, with fixed ropes and/or ladders, are to be taken seriously, especially in poor weather, and the exposure is often considerable.

Grade I climbing means no more than that the hands must be used (though this is also true of the ungraded 'protected' routes).

The highest grade in this book is a rock band in Piz Buin (I-II). This is no more difficult than the steepest parts of Tryfan, North Ridge, and in any case a rope will be carried on this walk because glaciers are crossed.

Snow. Many walks can involve walking on snow even in high summer, and traverses of steep snow can be very exposed. It is best to have an ice-axe of the 'old-fashioned', walking-stick length, so long as you know how to brake with it in the event of a slip. Many continental walkers are content with a spiked walking-stick (Alpenstock) or a ski-stick. These assist balance, but are no help in a slip. Alternatively use a pair of modern trekking poles.

Glaciers. Wherever there is the least danger of crevasses only roped parties of three or more should cross glaciers, and it is wise to become familiar with at least the simpler techniques of crevasse rescue in advance. Crampons also help and often save time by making step-cutting unnecessary. There are only a few walks involving serious glacier crossings in this book.

Clothing and Equipment

Weather can change quickly and drastically in the Austrian mountains. In all weathers warm clothing, waterproofs and a change of clothing should be carried. Carry water, snacks and emergency rations. (See under Huts with regard to other food.)

Good mountain boots with 'Vibram' type soles are essential, but nowadays these need not be desperately heavy. Do not rely on trainers, though they can be useful in the valleys. As boots may not be worn upstairs in huts some kind of slippers or 'Hüttenschuhe' are essential.

Pack-frames and rucksacks with exterior frames can be awkward and even dangerous on scrambly descents and are to be avoided. It is a good idea to have a light day-bag, or to be able to reduce the size of your main rucksack, for days out from huts.

If you are not carrying a full-length rope for glaciers or more difficult climbing than is described here, it is a good idea to carry a shorter length (say 10m) of a light-weight rope, and one or two slings and karabiners in case any member of the party gets into difficulties, or to lower or pull up a rucksack in some awkward place.

Always carry a compass and know how to use it in conjunction with your map.

Huts

The huts of the Alpine Club (and for this purpose there is no distinction between the German and Austrian Clubs, DAV and ÖAV) are mostly wardened; the wardens, who are normally really tenants, are responsible for catering, and it is from this that they make their living, as the bed-night money goes to the AV-Section. It is therefore not necessary to carry large quantities of food. Indeed, people who cook outside the hut but use its facilities are understandably and rightly very unpopular. It is a good idea, however, to carry tea, coffee and dried milk, as AV-members can obtain tea-water, (Teewasser) by the litre or half-litre plus use of cups for a very modest sum. 'Frühstück komplett' (complete breakfast) is usually the 'worst buy' and the majority of walkers generally carry bread or crispbread, butter, jam etc for breakfast, simply ordering 'Teewasser'. Most of the catering in huts is very good indeed and excellent value in the circumstances: all prices are agreed for the season in consultation with the AV-Section, bearing in mind the difficulty or otherwise of provisioning the hut in question.

Huts are also supposed to supply AV-members with 'Bergsteigeressen' (mountaineer's food) - a low-priced dish, which varies greatly, but which must have a certain nutritional value.

Sleeping accommodation in huts is of three kinds: 1) Beds. 2) Matratzenlager (or just 'Lager'). Only blankets and pillows are provided and one usually sleeps on a long communal 'bed', often filling the whole side of a room. 3) Notlager. This simply means 'emergency sleeping accommodation' and will probably be a mattress on a table or on the floor of the general living-room (Gaststube).

You *must* have a sheet sleeping bag.

Hut Categories

The AV divides huts into three categories:

Cat. I. Mountain huts usually at least 1 hour's walking from any mechanised transport. AV-members have 60% reduction in the price of sleeping accommodation (NOT food, except for the

Teeswasser and Bergsteigeressen privileges) and priority over non-members for beds and lager, usually up to 7 p.m. Age also has priority over youth. These huts can also be unwardened or mere bivouac boxes. No unwardened huts or bivouacs are used on the walks described.

Cat. II These are huts in very popular areas. They are particularly suitable for stays of several nights and for families. Unlike Category I huts, which are normally open only in summer (June or July to September or October), these are mostly open in winter also and can be reached by mechanical means (car or lift). The discount for AV members is usually at least 40%.

Cat. III These can be reached mechanically. They are primarily for day-visitors and offer less for over-nighters. The catering is in the style of normal hotel catering in the area. 20% reduction for AV-members.

Most of the huts used on the walks described are of Cat. I.

The Austrian Alpine Club: Section Britannia
The UK Branch of the Austrian Alpine Club (AAC), formerly known as 'Section England' and now more properly 'Section Britannia', was founded in 1948. Membership of it if you are walking in Austria is strongly to be recommended. Apart from the priorities and reductions at the huts, the Club sells its maps and guidebooks at a considerable reduction to its members, and can arrange insurance. Above all, if you are an AV-member in an AV hut, you 'belong'. (The address is: 2 Church Road, Welwyn Garden-City, Herts. AL8 6PT.)

Getting to Austria
Older books on Austria assumed the use of trains and buses. It is true at there are excellent continental trains to Austria and that many of the main bases, especially in the Inn valley, can still be easily reached by this means. Within Austria the Postbuses (which have absolute priority on roads) are also an excellent way of getting about. Many people, especially if in organised parties, fly to Austria and then rely on the local trains and buses. However, very many, probably a majority, of summer visitors now find that the most convenient (and in the end probably the most economical) form of holiday is to travel by private car and to camp. Many campsites will

14

charge only for the 'empty tent' (leeres Zelt) when you are away in the mountains, thus reducing the cost even further. In this book, therefore, campsites are mentioned and walks are usually described with the motorised visitor in mind.

Maps and Guidebooks

The sketch maps in this book are diagrammatic only and not drawn to scale. They MUST NOT be regarded as substitutes for properly scaled maps.

Apart from local maps, which can often be usefully bought after arrival, there are three series of maps which are the most important for the mountain walker.

1. *Alpenvereinskarten* (Alpine Club Maps). Usually 1:25,000. (AVK) These superb maps are the AV's own, designed for use in the mountains. Unless you want a map for skiing holidays as well as walking, do not buy the version with ski-routes, as these routes are printed more prominently than the paths and can be misleading.

2. *Kompass Wanderkarten* (Kompass Walking-Maps). 1:50,000 (K) Many walkers actually prefer these to the AVK maps, as the scale is familiar from our 1:50,000 OS Maps. But of course much detail is missing. Mountain paths are clearly marked.

3. *Freytag & Berndt Wanderkarten* 1:50,000 (FB). These are similar in scope to Kompass. Recommended.

   The list that follows suggests some of the most useful maps.

   AV =   Alpine Club Maps
   K   =   Kompass Maps
   FB =   Freytag & Berndt. (These maps are code-numbered WK, followed by a 3 figure number.)

LIST OF USEFUL MAPS

I *Bregenzerwaldgebirge (AVE Group 1)*
   FB WK 364

II *Allgäu Alps. (AVE Group 2)*
   AVK 2/1: K 3 (or 03 - 1:25,000): FB WK 363 (1:50,000)
   Beron. Landkreis Oberallgäu, Kleines Walsertal (Süd). 1:50,000

III Lechtal Alps (AVE Group 3b)
AVK 3/2, 3/3: K 24: FB WK 351 (1:50,000)

IV Karwendel (AVE Group 5)
AVK 5/1, 5/2: K 26: FB WK 322 (1:50,000)

V Kaisergebirge (AVE Group 8)
AVK 8: K 9; (& 09-1:25,000): FB WK 301 (1:50,000)

VI Berchtesgaden Alps (AVE Group 10)
K 14: FB WK 102 (1:50,000)
Plenk's Spezialführer, *Nationalpark Berchtesgaden*
(German text) contains useful large-scale maps.

VII Dachstein Gebirge (AVE Group 14)
AVK 14. For the Gosaukamm, either 14b, 1:25,000; or, better
14a, 1:10,000: K 20: FB WK 281 (1:50,000)

VIII Totes Gebirge (AVE Group 15)
AVK 15/1, 15/2: K 68, 69: FB WK 281, 082

IX Ennstaler Alps (AVE Group 16)
AVK 16: FB WK 6

X Rätikon (AVE Group 25)
K 32: FB WK 371 (1:50,000)

XI Silvretta (AVE Group 26)
AVK 26: K 41: FB WK 373 (1:50,000)

XII Ferwall (AVE Group 28)
AVK 3/2, 3/3: K 33, 41: FB WK 372 (1:50,000)

XIII Ötztal Alps (AVE Group 30)
AVK 30/1, 30/2, 30/3, 30/6: K 43: FB WK 251 (1:50,000)

XIV Stubai Alps (AVE Group 31)
AVK 31/1, 31/2: K 43: FB WK 241 (1:50,000)

XV Zillertal Alps (AVE Group 35)
AVK 35/1, 35/2: K 37: FB WK 152 (1:50,000)

XVI Venediger Group (AVE Group 36)
AVK 36: K 38, 46: FB WK 121, 123 (1:50,000)

XVII Villgratner Group (AVE Group 38)
AVK 41: FB WK 182

XVIII Granatspitz Group (AVE Group 39)
      AVK 39: K 46, 48: FB WK 122, 123 (1:50,000)

XIX Glockner Group (AVE Group 40)
      AVK 40: K 39, 48: FB WK 122

XX Schober Group (AVE 41)
      AVK 41: FB WK 181

XXI Goldberg Group (AVE Group 42)
      AVK 42: FB WK 191

XXII Ankogel Group (AVE Group 44)
      AVK 42: FB WK 191

XXIII Radstädter Tauern (AVE Group 45a)
      AVK 45/2: K 67: FB WK 201, 202

XXIV Schladminger Tauern (AVE Group 45b)
      AVK 45/2, 45/3: K 67: FB WK 201, 202

XXV Gailtaler Alps (Lienz Dolomites) (AVE Group 56)
      FB WK 182

GUIDEBOOKS

In English. There is no point in listing climbing guides in this book. The following books are those in English which have helped in planning the walks in this guidebook.

Philip Tallantire: *Felix Austria (Hut to Hut Touring Guides)*

Vol. I.	The Venediger region (1964)
Vol. II	The Zillertal Alps (1966)
Vol. III	Niederen and Hohen Tauern (1968)
Vol. IV	Pitztal - East and West (1966)

These books are now out of print.

They are now classics. They contain a wealth of historical, topographical, and even gastronomic and linguistic information. They are now three decades old, and some of their information is necessarily out-of-date. The standard of difficulty of walks is not always easy to judge from the descriptions.

Walter Pause: *100 Best Walks in the Alps* (Translated from German).

The 100 walks cover the whole Alpine area, but the Austrian Alps have their fair share, and several of the walks in this guidebook were suggested by Pause. There is only one page, a picture and a sketch map for each walk, and the description is not always detailed enough for use alone.

Jonathan Hurdle: *Walking Austria's Alps Hut to Hut* (Cordee)
    This describes 11 Tours of 4 to 11 days in length
Allan Hartley: *Hut-to-Hut in the Stubai Alps* (Cicerone Press)

In German. If you read German the Alpenverein guidebooks published by Bergverlag Rudolf Rother of Munich are superlatively good. Where a short guide (Kleiner Führer) exists it is better to buy this than the larger volume, not only because it is cheaper but also because it omits much that is useless to the walker (e.g. all climbs over Grade III) and concentrates upon the kind of routes used by mountain walkers, scramblers and climbers of modest ability and ambition.

Die Alpenvereinshütten (The AV-Huts) also published by Rother is well worth buying even if you do not read German. Section Britannia provides you with a duplicated glossary of essential words and abbreviations.

NOTE: *Latschen,* often mentioned in this book, is a kind of dwarf mountain pine which quickly becomes familiar to all walkers in the Eastern Alps.

Advice to Readers

Readers are advised that whilst every effort is taken by the author to ensure the accuracy of this guidebook, changes can occur which may affect the contents. It is advisable to check locally on transport, accommodation, shops etc. but even rights-of-way can be altered and, more especially overseas, paths can be eradicated by landslip, forest fires or changes of ownership.

    The publisher would welcome notes of any such changes.

I: The Bregenzerwaldgebirge
(AVE Group 1)

The Boundaries of the Group: Bodensee (Lake Constance) - Bregenzer Ache - Subersach - Schönenbach - Stogger Sattel - Rehmerbach - Au - Argenbach - Jochbach - Faschinajoch - Faschinabach - Lutz - Ill - Rhein - Bodensee.

As its name suggests this group consists of the mountains of the Bregenz Forest and it is, for British visitors, most naturally approached from the north-west: the Bodensee and the Rhine Valley.

For mountain walkers, however, the best base is not Bregenz but Dornbirn, which is in fact larger than the capital of the Vorarlberg and being an industrial town with a big trade fair in July and August does not on first approach look inviting, though the market place is attractive enough and the Red House, a fine half-timbered building of 1639 is a good restaurant. The Rappenlochschlucht, an impressive gorge, is worth a visit. It is on the Dornbirner Ache just beyond Gütle, a hamlet consisting of a textile mill of the Hämmerle family, some tied cottages and a guest-house. The Staufen See above the Schlucht offers a pleasant extension to this short walk.

To find the camping site, leave the motorway at "Dornbirn Süd" (south). The site, Camping in der Enz, lies to the SE of the town in the valley of the Dornbirner Ache. The nearby Grüner Baum is a convenient eating-out place.

1. THE HOHER FRESCHEN (2004m) (3 days)

Route: Dornbirn/Campsite - Kehlegg (c.790m) - Gschwendt Alm (1248m) - Lustenauer Hut (1250m) - Bregenzer Hut (1300m) - Weißefluh Hut (1375m) - Mörzelspitze (1830m) - Salzboden Kogel (1765m) - Binnen Alm (1724m) - Hoher Freschen (2004m) - Freschen Haus (1846m) - Göfiser Hohe (1788m) - Sünserweg - Blauer See - Sünser Joch - Sieben Hügel - Damüls.

This is the most obvious high-level walk from Dornbirn and certainly the best. The actual path begins at the little village of Kehlegg, which

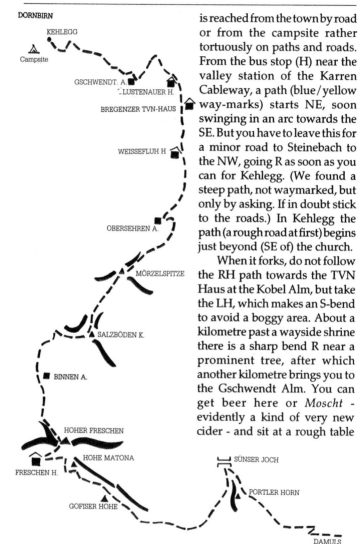

is reached from the town by road or from the campsite rather tortuously on paths and roads. From the bus stop (H) near the valley station of the Karren Cableway, a path (blue/yellow way-marks) starts NE, soon swinging in an arc towards the SE. But you have to leave this for a minor road to Steinebach to the NW, going R as soon as you can for Kehlegg. (We found a steep path, not waymarked, but only by asking. If in doubt stick to the roads.) In Kehlegg the path (a rough road at first) begins just beyond (SE of) the church.

When it forks, do not follow the RH path towards the TVN Haus at the Kobel Alm, but take the LH, which makes an S-bend to avoid a boggy area. About a kilometre past a wayside shrine there is a sharp bend R near a prominent tree, after which another kilometre brings you to the Gschwendt Alm. You can get beer here or *Moscht* - evidently a kind of very new cider - and sit at a rough table

I: BREGENZERWALD GEBIRGE WALK 1

20

outside. Inside the almhouse you can see all the equipment for cheese-making, no longer in use, and beyond the small fenced 'garden' you may encounter friendly Haflingers.

Shortly beyond and above the Gschwendt Alm you cross a small pass, then walk down easily, NNE, to the Hochälpele Alm, a large, well-kept house with many outbuildings. In 1988 this was empty. It is the property of a century-old Dornbirn dynasty of textile manufacturers with world-wide connections, the Hämmerle family, who used it as a kind of holiday home for their employees until so much damage was done that the scheme was ended. After this pass a little chapel, the Benedikt Kapelle and a small lake, then continue up and down muddily through woods to the Lustenauer Hut: an easy 3$^{1}/_{2}$hrs from the campsite, including refreshment break.

This hut takes its name from Lustenau, a town on the east bank of the Rhine a few kilometres west of Dornbirn. Thus, unlike many, indeed most, huts of the Alpenverein, it has strong local roots and indeed serves as a local pub for the lads and girls of Schwarzenberg in the valley below, who ignore the usual "quiet at ten" rule of Alpine huts and keep it up until midnight, sometimes to the annoyance of members of the Lustenau Alpenverein Section who want "Hüttenruhe" at 10pm. But these locals do enable the warden to make a modest living even though 'overnighters' like us are very few: there were only five altogether the night we stayed, and of course the actual 'bed-night' fees go to the Alpenverein.

From the Lustenau Hut the path (No. 201, and also part of the European Long-distance Path No. 4) starts nearly due south, climbing gently through largely wooded country to the Bregenzer Hut (1300m) of the Naturfreunde (Friends of Nature, TVN), then about a kilometre further past the same club's Weißefluh Hut at 1375m. In several big zig-zags the path now drops, short-cutting a rough road, to a muddy area where there is a hunting lodge, and continues to the Untersehren Alm. This is all through green country along what is essentially a very broad, gently undulating 'ridge' - if one may extend that word to include this series of wide saddles.

Beyond this alm you begin to climb more steeply apparently towards the Obersehren Alm at 1519m, but before you reach the alm the path swings left and climbs steadily round a big 'cwm' to bring you out on a really fine ridge - the first bit of manifestly 'mountain' walking on this route. The path skirts the Leuenkopf (1830m) and then climbs the Mörzelspitze (also 1830m), the first big 'top' of the day. You are now about half-way in distance to the Freschen Haus, but the second half is much more energetic than the first, as you can now see for yourself. The dark north face of the Hoher Freschen is already a challenging goal. Before leaving the Mörzelspitze do savour the view to the west, where the mountains of Switzerland tower up beyond the Rhine Valley.

The path now drops some 400m, only to climb again to the Salzboden Kogel (1765m). Then once again you lose height, by-passing the Allenhof Alm to avoid losing even more. For a time the path is in a sort of gully, offering welcome shade on a hot day, then continues easily over high meadows to the Binnen Alm (1724m) where refreshments are available. Soon after this you are on the almost knife-edge ridge leading to the steep, narrow, north arête of the Hoher Freschen, protected in parts by fixed ropes - a dramatic and worthy climb to the day's high spot at just over 2000m. Notices here inform you that the north ridge you have just climbed, and the west ridge, are both *Nur für geübte* (only for the experienced) unless with a guide. To the north there is a fine retrospective view of the latter part of the day's route, and you may not be sorry to see that there is an easy walk from the summit to the Freschen Haus about a mile away at 1846m. This is in a magnificent situation with views of the Upper Rhine Valley, the Swiss mountains, and, to the south, the Rätikon and other Austrian mountain groups. There is a delightful alpine garden and a modern chapel to St. Bernard, patron saint of mountaineers, with a fine mural of the saint. Just below is the Obere Saluver Alm with a large almhouse for cattle and herdsman.

After a night here start almost due east, then south, skirting the Hohe Matona - though this summit, at 1997m only 7m lower than the Hoher Freschen, is well worth a visit. The path continues SE above high north-facing cliffs, to the Göfiser Höhe (1788m, marked by a cross). Paths come up here from the Göfis Alm (1746m) that then lead down to the Rankweil-Damüls road. The whole area is remarkable for its flora.

Continue on 201, now called the Stechweidweg. To the north is a great basin where everything - alm, lake or pass - is called *Süns* or

I: BREGENZERWALD GEBIRGE WALK 2

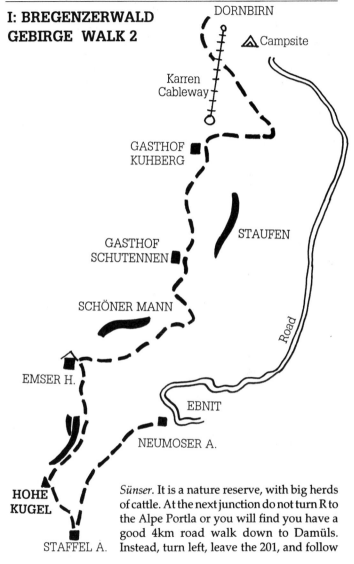

DORNBIRN

△ Campsite

Karren
Cableway

GASTHOF
KUHBERG

STAUFEN

GASTHOF
SCHUTENNEN

SCHÖNER MANN

Road

EMSER H.

EBNIT

NEUMOSER A.

HOHE
KUGEL

STAFFEL A.

Sünser. It is a nature reserve, with big herds of cattle. At the next junction do not turn R to the Alpe Portla or you will find you have a good 4km road walk down to Damüls. Instead, turn left, leave the 201, and follow

23

the Sünser Weg under the Portler Kogel and the Portler Horn. (Don't take the left fork down to the Süns Alm.) After a tarn called the Blauer See you reach the Sünser Joch where you make a hairpin bend and walk SE on the east side of the Portler Horn. The most direct route into Damüls is to fork left on a blue waymarked path across the Sieben Hügeln (Seven Hills). Damüls is primarily a ski-resort. There is no Alpenverein or similar hut, but many guest-houses.

(Owing to deteriorating weather we ended the walk here and took the bus back to Dornbirn. The continuation should be to either the Gasthof Edelweiß or the Hofstätten Hut and thence to Au or Mellau, again to catch the bus home. The cable-way could be used to save the climb out of Damüls.)

(Note: the Freschen House can also be reached on paths from Rankweil.)

(1988)

2. HOHE KUGEL (1645m)

Route: Ebnit - Schneewald Alm - Hohe Kugel - Emser Hut (1272m) - Gasthof Schutennen - Gasthof Kühberg (950m) - campsite.

Take the bus to Ebnit, through dramatic road tunnels. Ebnit has been partly 'developed' as a 'holiday village'. Take the blue-waymarked path from the Heumoser Alm. The start may not be easy to find. Go steeply up SW with many zig-zags. Watch the signs in the vicinity of the Schneewald Alm. Be prepared for a hairpin bend near the Staffel Alm. The Kugel Alpe is just below the summit. Not a thrilling top but with interesting views across the deep valley to the Hoher Freschen.

Walk north along the broad ridge to point 1572m (don't fork left) and continue down to the Emser Hut, privately owned, where you might be ripped off for your bread and cheese. Now follow red waymarks clockwise round the Schöner Mann until you join a motor-road which you follow to the busy and car-infested Gasthof Schutennen. From here take the farthest left of several paths: the Staufen (1465m) is on your right. The next landmark, the Gasthof Kühberg, will doubtless be full of people who have come up on the Karren Cableway. To avoid descending on this, take the next path to the right, then left on blue waymarks. This eventually passes under the cable-way and finishes on the road not far from its valley-station near the campsite.

II : The Allgäu Alps
(AVE Group 2)

The Name: The group takes its name from the Allgäu, the SW corner of Bavaria, whose boundary with Austria its main chain forms.

Boundaries of the Group: The alpine foothills - the R. Lech via the Forggensee and Füssen as far as Warth - the Krummbach - the Hochtannberg Pass - the Seebach - the Bregenzer Ache as far as Rehmen - the Rehmerbach - the Stogger Sattel - the Osterguntenbach - the Schönenbach - the Subersach - the Bregenzer Ache - the alpine foothills.

The main range of the group runs NE-SW and forms the Austro-German frontier east of the Iller valley.

British walkers approaching from the north will probably, in fact base themselves in Germany. Oberstdorf is the obvious base, but campers will find the campsite small, crowded and rather miserably hemmed in by a triangle of roads and railway. The site at Sonthofen resists all attempts at pegging and is suitable only for caravans. But Buchner's Campingplatz at Bühl on the shores of the Alpsee near Immenstadt is excellent and worth the longer drive to the mountains.

The hills of 1100-1500m near Immenstadt provide a wealth of very pleasant rambles should you not yet be fit or should the weather be second rate. e.g. Zaumberg - the Thäler Höhe (1166m) - Wiedemannsdorf: or; the Immenstädter Horn (1490m), a rewarding little summit - the Kemptener Naturfreunde Haus - the Geschwender Horn (1450m).

There is also one major mountain walk near Immenstadt, the Nagelfluh (Walk 1). This and the walk to the Kempter Hut (Walk 2) are part of the E5 European Long-distance Footpath from the Bodensee to the Adriatic, popularised among German walkers through a TV programme about 1982-3.

1. THE NAGELFLUHKETTE

This is a 12km ridge (as the Alpine chough flies) with five major summits.

There is a 2-stage chair-lift (Mittag Chair-lift) at Immenstadt, the NE end, and a gondola-lift (the Hochgrat lift) at the SW end. Bus services to the SW end are bad, so to do the walk in a day and still return to base you must plant a car at the far end before setting out. Otherwise stay at the Staufner Haus (1600m Cat. II) near the top of the Hochgrat lift. A third possibility is to take the walk in two bites as described

a) Mittagberg (1451m) - Stuiben (1749m)

Take the Mittag chair-lift to Mittagberg: the walk up is an unrelenting drag of 400-500m. Walk mildly SW to the Bärenkopf (1463m), an unremarkable outcrop with a cross. Continue in the same direction. As you approach the Steineberg (1660m) the ridge becomes narrow and the summit cross looks inaccessible above cliffs and crags. The path drops steeply, then climbs steeply.

(There is an alternative more scrambly route, *Nur für Geübte* 'Only for the experienced'.)

The path passes *below* the summit ridge, then back-tracks to the cross. ($1^{1}/_{2}$hrs from the Mittagberg.) Dramatic view back and down.

From this point the path is interesting and follows a real ridge, with one easy rock-traverse down a crag. Soon after this, drop to 1500m and then climb Stuiben (1749m). This includes a quite exciting bit of rock with fixed ropes. ($1^{1}/_{2}$hrs from Steineberg.) Stuiben summit is a Mecca or honey-pot and you will doubtless want to get away from it.

(There is a considerable drop to quite a low pass between Stuiben and the next major summit, the Buralpkopf (1772m).)

Descend from Stuiben on the north side - no path on map at first, but then follow good tracks slightly west of north to the Mittelberg Alm, a beautiful almhouse full of character, old farm implements, etc. A limited choice of refreshments.

There is a good and quite picturesque road from here down the valley back to Immenstadt, about 5km.

b) Hochgrat (1832m) - Buralpkopf (1772m)

From Immenstadt or Bühl drive to the valley station of the Hochgrat gondola-lift via Oberstaufen, Weissach, Höfen and Steibis. The gondola gives you a lift of something like 800m! A big restaurant etc. at the top. The Staufner Haus (1600m Cat. II) is just a little lower, to the SW. Walk up easily NE to the Hochgrat summit (1832m), then drop down a good ridge path to the Brunnenscharte (1624m). Up again at once to 1754m (nameless), and drop yet again: then up to the very dramatic summit of the Rindalphorn (1822m). It is a tiny summit, the best 'top' in the whole chain *(Kette)*. Precipitous to the north, it justifies its name (Rind=cattle) by the grazing on

IMMENSTADT

ALPSEE

1a

1a

Mittagberg

Steineberg

Stuiben

Buralpkopf

EIBELE-ALM

1b

Rindalphorn

II: THE ALLGÄU ALPS
NAGELFLUHKETTE

Hochgrat

STAUFNER HAUS

the southern slopes.

The next drop is very steep to a picturesque and nameless col, and steep again the climb to the Gündleskopf (no height on map), then easily to the Buralpkopf (1772m), a good hour from the Rindalphorn. If you go a little beyond the Buralpkopf you can see clearly the route over the Sedererwände and the low col between here and Stuiben.

(If you have no car to return to you could without difficulty go down to this col and walk from there to the Mittelberg Alm as in Walk 1a.)

If you are going no further and have left a car below the Hochgrat, return same route.   (1983)

2. THE KEMPTER HUT (1846m Cat. I)

(Also spelt Kemptner. *The hut is run by the Kempten Section of the AV.)*
Like the Nagelfluh, the walk to the Kempter Hut is part of the E5 European
Long-distance Footpath, Lindau-Bolzano-the Adriatic.

If in a car, avoid the centre of Oberstdorf (fearful one-way system)
but instead take the by-pass signposted for the Fellhorn cable-lift,
and find a big long-stay car park at Renksteg at a crossroad just
south of the town. There is a made road, not open to public traffic,
all the way to Spielmannsau (guest-house and youth hostel). You
may also ride to this point from Oberstdorf in a horse-drawn
'surrey'! If walking, it is probably more pleasant to fork left on a
footpath on the east side of the river rather than to stay on the road
on the west side. The views of the valley-head and mountains in
front of you are attractive.

Above Spielmannsau the track continues as far as the valley
station of the goods cable-way (Materialseilbahn) for the Kempter
Hut, then suddenly becomes very much a mountain path, threatened
by stonefall or avalanche according to season. At one point the
whole path has been swept away, presumably by spring floods, and
there are long ladders to help descent into a deep gully that has to
be crossed. At point 1232m, (map) there is a fork in the gorge. The
path goes left to follow the Sperrbach. Cross this soon on a bridge.
Zig-zag up a bank appropriately called *Am Knie* (At the Knee), to
avoid an impassable section of gorge. Then the path drops a little,
crosses the stream to its left (true right) side and climbs the Sperrbach
Tobel, its head dominated by the shapely Muttlerkopf (2366m). The
'Tobel' is a dramatic gorge which can be mercilessly hot and
windless. Far above you will see the goods-cable serving the hut:
don't let this discourage you, for the top station is at 1914m, the best
part of a kilometre from the hut and 70m higher.

On emerging from the Tobel it is therefore a pleasure to see the
hut quite near and only 100m above you. The path swings round to
the right to reach it. It is a large hut, sleeping over 300 people, built
in 1892 and enlarged several times; much frequented because of its
importance for the long-distance footpath and the Heilbronner
Way (Walk 4).   (1983)

3.   THE MUTTLERKOPF (2366m)

The mountain that beckoned us up the Sperrbach Tobel is the nearest and easiest summit to climb from the Kempter Hut (see Walk 2).
Start due south on path 438, still part of the E5. At point 1880m fork left on Path 432 up to the Oberer Mädelejoch (2033m) on the Austro-German border. Pause for views: SW, the Kratzer (2424m); due east the Krottenkopf (2657m), a very popular summit from the Kempter Hut; W the Kempter Hut itself; and south, the Lech valley near Holzgau. Continue a few yards on 432, then take a branch sharp left and a good zig-zag path takes you easily up the SSE (Austrian) face to the summit - also on the national frontier. Views as from the col, but greatly enhanced: NE the Öfnerspitze (2576m), NNW the incredible Krottenspitzen (2383m); W the hut, the Sperrbach Tobel and the Land-Rover track from the hut to the top of the goods-cable. (Query: was the Land-Rover originally delivered by helicopter?) To the south we have our first panorama of the Eastern Alps in Austria: the Lechtal Alps from the Valluga to the Parseier Spitze.

After savouring all this to the full, return same way. (Hut to summit, $1^{3/4}$hrs.)   (1983)

4.   THE KEMPTER HUT (1846m Cat. I) - THE WALTENBERGER HAUS (2085m Cat. I), VIA THE HEILBRONNER WAY (Part).

From the Kempter Hut (Walk 2) follow 438 (E5) towards the Mädelejoch, but before reaching it fork right and you will soon be on the frontier at point 2096m. You are now on the Heilbronner Way on the Austrian side. Glance back at the NE view towards the Muttlerkopf (2366m), Öfnerspitze (2587m) and the Krottenspitze (2383m), not to mention the Krottenkopf (2675m). It is a pleasantly rising path with glimpses NE into Bavaria. Soon you will see the vast valley of the Schochenalp Bach with the Hohes Licht (2652m) at its head. The path traverses easily around the slopes of this valley under the jagged Kratzer (2424m) and then towards the Mädelegabel (2645m) and the pyramidal Trettachspitze (2595m).

There is one 'bad step' consisting in fact of two linked rock steps with a slack fixed rope: very awkward to negotiate. Soon above this is the safe and easy Schwarzmilz Ferner (glacier). This leads up to a spur, a fine viewpoint, and a few yards beyond this is the (eastern) Bockkarscharte (2523m), a dramatic rocky pass. (3hrs from the hut.)

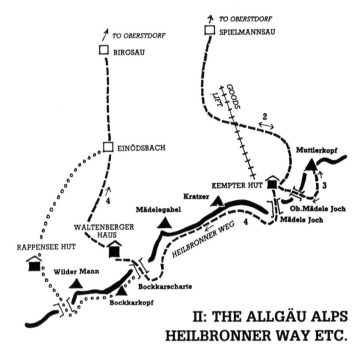

II: THE ALLGÄU ALPS
HEILBRONNER WAY ETC.

(Here begins the *Hohenweg* section of the Heilbronner Way, a 'protected route' (Via Ferrata) with fixed ropes etc, over the knife-edge Bockkarkopf (2608m) and the Wilder Mann (2577m) to the Rappensee Hut (2091m Cat. I), another large hut, sleeping 332 at a pinch.)

Our route drops NW into the Vorderes Bockkar - steep, unstable rock with fixed ropes, followed by scree, to the Waltenberger Haus (2085m Cat. I). The sign says 50mins. Don't believe it unless you are very agile on an insecure descent! The hut is small and friendly, set on a grassy eminence with a minute helicopter pad - only for gas bottles and the like: the warden has to carry the rest up on his back. His menu, using a minimum number of different ingredients in a multitude of different ways is ingenious and tasty.

The path down has a very dramatic section across the face of a high, practically vertical rock-band with exciting views up into a

Vorderes Bockkar and Waltenberger Haus

huge, madly steep, snow-filled 'gully', the Schneeloch (snow-hole) below the Rotgundspitze (2484m). Afterwards, walking north below the rock-band, you can look up at fine waterfalls. An easy valley path leads to the hamlet of Einödsbach, the most southerly permanently inhabited place in Germany, with a charming little church.

(The path from the Rappensee Hut also comes down here.)

From Einödsbach (the very name implies loneliness and isolation) easy walking to Birgsau. Be sure to catch the bus here (it went at 11 a.m. in 1983) to Renksteg car park or through to Oberstdorf, as the road-walk would have nothing to recommend it.

(1983)

III: The Lechtal Alps
(AVE Group 3b)

Boundaries of the Group: The R. Lech from Lech to Reutte - Porta Claudia - Nassereith - R. Gurgl to its junction with the R. lnn - R. lnn to Landeck - R. Sanne, then the R. Rosanna to St. Anton - Arlberg Pass - R. Rauzbach to Stuben - Flexen Pass - the Zürser Bach to Lech.

The Lechtal Alps are, on account of their extremely complex geological formations, both attractive and serious. Within an area of about 1000sq km are contained nearly 500 peaks of over 2000m - easy and very difficult summits of similar altitude often standing close to each other. Forty-five high-level lakes and 8 mini glaciers add character to the scenery. Although the group constitutes part of the Northern Limestone Alps, the routes often include much friable and shaley rock. Dangerously steep grass slopes are another characteristic of the group - on some of them hay-making demands the use of crampons: no wonder if such slopes are nowadays used only as pasture!

The walks here described avoid some of the most difficult routes, but most are to be treated seriously. Even in August an ice-axe may not be superfluous, especially in a year of heavy or late snow.

The approaches from the north by road are: from Bregenz, over the dramatic Hochtannberg Pass (1679m) to Lech; from Füssen via Reutte up the deeply-cut Lechtal itself to Lech; or from Reutte via Lermoos over the Fern Pass to Imst for southern approaches.

1. LECH TO FLIRSCH

Route: via Stuttgarter Hut (2303m) (Cat. I) - Leutkircher Hut (2252m) (Cat. I) - Kaiserjoch Haus (2306m) (Cat. I) - Ansbacher Hut (2376m) (Cat. I).

Lech is a commercialised and characterless ski-resort where overnight accommodation should not be difficult to find in summer.

Krottenspitzen from Muttlerkopf, Allgäu
Kaisertal with Scheffauer from Höhenweg, Kaisergebirge

III: THE LECHTAL ALPS WALK 1

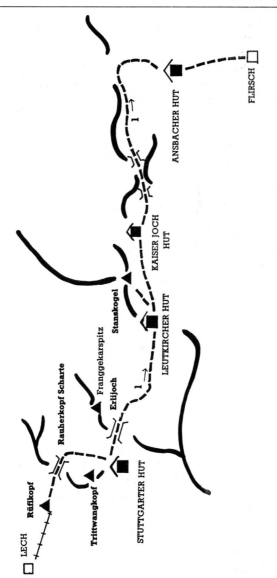

LECH

Rüfikopf

Trittwangkopf

Rauherkopf Scharte

Franggekarspitz

Ertljoch

STUTTGARTER HUT

1 →

Stanskogel

LEUTKIRCHER HUT

KAISER JOCH HUT

1 →

ANSBACHER HUT

FLIRSCH

33

Most walkers wisely start by taking the Rüfikopf cable-car, which lifts one painlessly from 1450m to 2362m - 900m of ascent! - straight to the joys of high-level walking: indeed, there is an initial loss of 200m of height, through a large, shallow basin, the Ochsengümple followed by an ascent to the Rauherkopfscharte (2415m). From here the Stuttgarter Hut is visible and soon reached. (Care in mist: the hut is not *on* the Krabach Joch but about 200m south of it.) From the cable-car, 1¹/₂hrs.

It is early enough in the day to take in a summit without the heavy bag. The easiest - but it is rewarding - is the grassy Trittwangkopf (2483m), the hut's *Hausberg*, whose top is reached 30mins from the hut. (Its other sides are precipitous, though there *is* a route along the ridge to the Gümplespitze: 1hr, Grade II climbing!) From here the first sections of tomorrow's choice of route can be clearly seen.

(Due south from the Stuttgarter Hut the Boschweg leads to the Ulmer Hut (2285m) on the southern slopes of the Valluga (2809m), St. Anton's heavily mechanised ski-mountain, and directly above the Arlberg Pass. This route involves a fixed rope at the Trittscharte (2580m) and there may be steep, hard snow also. The continuation from the Ulmer Hut to the Leutkircher Hut is slightly more difficult - Grade B.)

SE from the Stuttgarter Hut the path direct to the Leutkircher Hut can be seen from Trittwangkopf as far as the Erli-Joch (2430m) with the steep and heavily buttressed cliffs of the Fanggekarspitze (2640m) to its left. This is the more beautiful route, though its views are less open than from the Ulmer Hut route. It is not as much used as the route via the Ulmer Hut and is recommended by the German guidebook to anyone who wants beauty and 'is not averse to little adventures'. The guidebook time - without adding a summit - is 4hrs, and the grade can rise to B on the Stapfetobel section after rain or snow, or when there is ice.

From the Stuttgarter Hut the going is easy as far as the Erli-Joch, and unless time presses an ascent of the Fanggekarspitze (leaving bags at the joch) is worthwhile. The actual way up is uninteresting, on scree, steep at first, and the summit is described as 'somewhat boring' in the guidebook, but the splendid close-ups of the magnificent dolomitic pinnacles on the west face, and the extensive views even beyond the Valluga to the Ferwall, with the serrated ridge of the Kuchenspitze, far outweigh any alleged tedium.

The descent from the Erli-Joch to the Erlach Alm (1919m) may involve a traverse on steep snow near the top. During this descent one can begin to assess conditions on the path as it crosses the north side of the Stapfetobel. After crossing the Almajurbach by a plank bridge the path traverses an unstable mixture of mud and stone chips followed by a horizontal crack with a sloping floor. There are two gullies to be crossed, probably snow-filled, and some sections are liable to be affected by landslips. In a bad year (e.g. 1972) these can make the path impassable. Enquire at the Stuttgarter Hut before leaving. Soon after this tricky section the path is joined by that from the Ulmer Hut (and the Kapall Lift above St. Anton) and the friendly and comfortable Leutkircher Hut can be seen.

As the route from here to the Kaiserjoch Hut takes only about 2hrs, mostly across botanically rich alpine meadows, the ascent of the Stanskogel (2757m) en route is to be recommended. Don't leave your rucksack at the fork, but carry it up beyond the Kirschpleiskopf (2549m), as an alternative route back to the main (601) path between this and the Stanskogel, saves some retracing of steps. As far as the top of the western shoulder of the Stanskogel there are no difficulties, but the traverse across the crumbly south flank below the rock towers of the summit ridge requires care and is Grade I climbing - you have to use your hands. An easy path to the summit follows. The 'summit cross' is on a slightly lower subsidiary top, where it is visible from the valley. The view is stupendous. South from the main summit the Hoher Riffler provides a superb backdrop to the cross, its shape repeating that of the cross's rock plinth like some vast Brockenspectre. From the cross St. Anton can be seen deep in the Rosanna valley, while to the east the central Lechtal mountains present a wild tangle of steeply pointed tops.

Return to the main path either by the same route or more steeply in zig-zags between the Hirschpleiskopf and the Stanskogel, and continue to the Kaiserjoch Hut, a tiny hut set windily on the pass of that name. Some degree of sure-footedness is required by the final lap down to the hut. In 1975 the hut warden was permanently, but amiably, drunk, while one long-suffering woman, apparently his wife, did *all* the cooking on one small Calor gas cooker. No wonder the menu was 'spaghetti or spaghetti'. And half the company had to go to bed to leave room for the other half to eat. (And half must have slept on the floor: we, after much difficulty, got the last two places on the Matratzen-Lager.)

The climax of this walk is the section from the Kaiserjoch Hut to the Ansbacher Hut, described in Groth's guidebook as a 'two-lakes way with question-marks'. East from the hut a traverse, mostly on grass and scree, but perhaps involving snow, on the southern slopes of the Grieskopf to the Kridlonscharte (2365m) where a wonderful view to the north suddenly bursts upon the eye. Directly below lies the Hintersee, a deeply green-blue eye, and behind it rises the shapely Aples Pleis Spitzen (2655m). Our path now traverses above this on the slopes of the Kridlonkar, towards the symmetrical pyramid of the Vordersee Spitze (2888m), then climbs steeply in zig-zags to the Hinterseejoch (2484m). From this narrow, rocky pass we can see both the Hintersee and the Vordersee.

(The continuation of the traverse path, if one does not go up to the Hinterseejoch, leads to the Simms Hut (Cat. I) (2004m), NW of the Wetter Spitze. The route is not easy and involves, among other things, 30m of descent on fixed rope. From the Simms Hut there is a path, not involving difficulties, but including over 1000m regaining of height, to the Ansbacher Hut.)

After a steep drop of some 150m towards the Vordersee we take the Theodor Haas Way, a high-level route made on the south cliff of the Vordersee Spitze: a wonderful path going into the gullies and out on to the spurs, sometimes grotty, sometimes rocky, sometimes with fixed rope, more often without, sometimes reaching easy exposed 'Moderate' standard, though graded only A by Groth.

The Alperschonjoch (2301m) when it is reached is wide and bare, though with fine views of fantastic summits of strangely distorted rock to the NE. The path from the Simms Hut joins ours here, we cross a final pass, the Flarsch Joch (2515m) and descend south to the Ansbacher Hut with the Hoher Riffler once more facing us across the Rosanna valley. The hut stands on a broad spur with extensive views up and down the valley. The guidebook time from the Kaiserjoch is 5hrs: allow more to enjoy it.

From the hut the descent of some 1200m to Flirsch is steep and often slippery. (A slightly longer alternative leads to Schnann.) If your transport has been left at Lech you can catch a train to St. Anton and from there a bus to Lech. If you have to wait, the railway station restaurant at St. Anton, familiar to economical skiers, is better than most of its kind. (1975)

(The continuation of the Lechtal High Level route is as follows:
EiTHER

a) The Augsberg High-Level way to the Augsburger Hut. (Cat. I) 8-10hrs! Very serious. Only to be attempted by experienced, strong parties with rope and ice-axes.

OR

b) To the Memminger Hut. (Cat. I) 5$^{1/2}$hrs. No extraordinary difficulties.

c) Memminger Hut - Augsburg Hut. Quite serious. No further route E from this hut. (Cat. I).

d) Memminger Hut - Württemberger Haus (Cat. I). 4$^{1/2}$hrs. No extraordinary difficulties.

e) Württemberger Haus - Steinsee Hut. (Cat. I) 4hrs. One tricky section of ascent.

f) Steinsee Hut - Hanauer Hut. (Cat. I) 2$^{1/2}$-3$^{1/2}$hrs. Choice of 2 routes. No extraordinary difficulties.

g) Alternatively there is a direct route from the Württemberger Haus to the Hanauer Hut. 5$^{1/2}$hrs. No extraordinary difficulties except for a loose fixed rope.

h) Hanauer Hut - Muttekopf Hut. (Cat. I). Care on the Kübelwände. Some fixed rope below Muttekopf Scharte. 1000m loss of height to be regained en route.

i) Muttekopf Hut - Anhalter Hut. (Cat. I). 4$^{1/2}$hrs. No extraordinary difficulties.)

2. THE MUTTEKOPF (2777m) 'Hausberg' of Imst

Although walkers on the eastern section of the Lechtal high-level route can easily - an extra hour - include the Muttekopf while walking from the Hanauer Hut to the Muttekopf Hut, it is well worth a visit for its own sake.

Imst is a little town totally unlike Lech. It is old, with archaeological finds dating back to the Bronze and Iron Ages. It has thereafter a continuous history. Although it is a tourist and ski centre it also has flourishing, though unobtrusive, industry and so is a community in its own right, a place where you meet natives as well as holidaymakers. Of its two campsites, Imst West is quieter and less crowded than the one at the open-air swimming pool.

There are three mechanised ways of starting off for the Muttekopf Hut (1934m): (Cat. I)

1) to drive 10km to the Latschen Hut (Obermarkter Alm) at 1700m and walk up the valley, climbing 200m.

2) to catch the minibus to Sonneck (1030m) and take the first stage of the chair-lift to the Untermarkter Alm at 1500m. From here a good path (for good heads only) cuts along the north side of the hill and reaches the hut in 30mins.

3) as for 2, but take also the newer, second stage of the chair-lift to the Drischlhaus (2050m). (This is a pleasant place to visit anyway, with good scenic walking uphill from it.) From here a newer path is cut out of the cliff *down* to the Muttekopf Hut. Back in the 1960s this hut was remarkable in that it had an Englishwoman - widow of an Austrian guide - as warden.

From the hut much of the walk as far as the Muttekopf Scharte (2661m) is up a bare, stony valley, steep in places, with zig-zags.

(At 2309m a fork to the left leads to the Imster Hohenweg. This goes over the Larsengrat back to Imst, but takes about 8hrs from hut to town. Do not underestimate it! Ask at the hut if in doubt.)

The last 100ft or so to the Scharte consists of slabs protected by a fixed rope, and from the Scharte to the summit is easy walking on a bare, broad, stony ridge reminiscent of the Glyders. There is a large cross on the summit and views down towards the Pitztal and Kaunergrat to the south.

On the return walk it is pleasant not to use the upper chair-lift

III: THE LECHTAL ALPS
WALKS 2-4 & 9

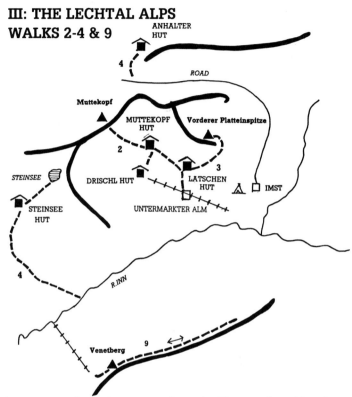

but to enjoy the high pastures above the Untermarkter Alm. An agreeable way to walk back to Imst (though not the shortest) is via Gunglgrün.

3. VORDERER PLATTEINSPITZE (2565m)

A fine viewpoint - but with hardly room for more than two on the rocky summit.

Start from either the Muttekopf Hut or the Latschen Hut. Groth's German guidebook describes the former - here we give the latter. The upper part of the route is the same for both. From the Latschen

Hut, north (the start may not be quite clear) to a waterfall, then up the path, the Platteinsteig (red/white waymarks) on to the Plattein meadows. It becomes steep and red-tipped sticks mark the way to a scree-field. Cross this and you will find an exciting sort of miniature gorge - or spectacularly gigantic crack - which leads into an enormous gully, from which the summit is visible. Up the gully on rather loose scree through pinnacled rock-scenery recalling the Quiraing. At the head of the gully you are on a small saddle between an outer curtain of rock and the summit pile behind. Pause to appreciate the awesome and fantastic scenery that surrounds you. The summit cross is hidden again. The path now traverses the north side of the mountain, rising gradually between the rock above and the scree below to the foot of a fixed rope.

The rest of the ascent is a glorious scramble reasonably well protected by fixed rope, but graded I-II. Up a fixed rope, traverse left, up a fairly steep gully with fixed rope; a loose slope with a slack rope to a tiny col, short descent to a loose gully: up this on to a narrow ridge and a slab, exposed but not steep, with fixed rope; then a ledge leading to the tiny summit with cross and book. Apart from the extensive views to south and east the situation is most impressive in respect of the great Cuillin-like ridge NW up to the Hinterer Plattein (2639m) - but this Grade III climb is beyond our present scope. Put your name in the summit book - it won't contain many! - and retrace your way. Care is needed in the great gully.   (1969)

4. OTHER WALKS FROM IMST

Obviously Imst can be used as a base for the whole eastern section of the Lechtal high-level route. The less ambitious may do sections - using the excellent train service in the valley for returning home. Even visiting individual huts can be worthwhile.

The Anhalter Hut (2042m) (Cat. I) can be reached in $4^{1/2}$hrs from the Muttekopf Hut over the Scharnitzsattel and the Steinjöchl, or from the Hahntennjoch (1884m) - to which you can drive - over the Steinjöchl only. And from the Steinjöchl the Maldongrat (2252m) (the most westerly 'top' of the Heiterwand) can be ascended - but it is harder than it looks. Keep off in ice and snow!   (1975)

More rewarding is the **Steinsee Hut** (2029m) (Cat. I). Catch the morning train from Imst to Schönwies (736m) There is a fine gorge of the Starkenbach early in the walk, but later the going is steep. Allow at least 4¹/₂hrs. The friendly, family-run hut possesses a tin crusher provided by a donation from the 'Sektion England' of the Austrian Alpine Club. The situation among dolomitic cliffs is impressive, and the Steinsee itself very beautiful. (For routes to other huts see notes to Walk 1.) An alternative end to the descent leads to Zams and includes walking through a tunnel. (1975)

III. THE LECHTAL ALPS WALK 5

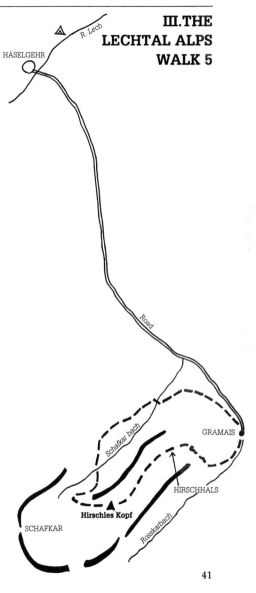

5. HIRSCHLES KOPF (2952m)

This and the following three walks are based on the valley of the River Lech. We camped at Häselgehr in appalling weather (1987); hence the modesty of the walks described.

Walk or drive to Gramais (1328m) 6km SSE of Häselgehr (1008m) Start up the Roßkarbach, but soon

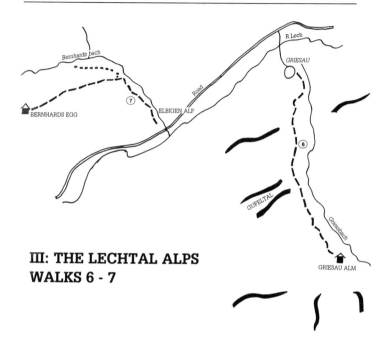

III: THE LECHTAL ALPS
WALKS 6 - 7

go right (NW) climbing steeply through woods on to the Hirschhals (The Deer's Neck) at about 1650m, then more gently (SW) up open pastures to the Hirschleskopf (2952m) with its modest summit cross. Follow a good path SW, but bear right near point 2008m. (Straight on is a high-level path to the Roßkar.) This takes you across the open slopes of the Schafkar (sheep corrie). Do not go up to the Schafkarsee (probably pathless), but follow waymarks down steep grass slopes (NE) into the valley of the Schafkarbach/Alpbach. Cross the river (probably with difficulty), and follow the path back to Gramais.

6. GRIESBACH ALP (1475m)

A road walk (unsurfaced) with impressive scenery.

Start at Griesau about 2km up the valley from Häselgehr and take

42

a private road due south. The scenery is dramatic, especially where you cross the Gufeltal, a vast double gully. Refreshments are available at the Alp, and you *may* even be greeted with a complimentary schnaps! Return the same way. (1987)

7. BERNARDSEGG (1802m)

Elbigenalp has been inhabited since 954AD and the church dates from 1399. The 'Totentanz' (Dance of Death) in the churchyard chapel is the work of the 'universal genius' Anton Falger (1791-1871). There is a startling charnel-house in the chapel basement.

Start at Elbigenalp about 4km up the valley from Häselgehr, taking the path on the (true) right of the Bernhardsbach above the klamm. After about 1km go sharp left (1259m). If you find yourself opposite the steep Balschtebach you know you have missed the turning. The original path has been destroyed by the building of the forestry road, but you may still find several steep short-cuts. Eventually you join the original line of the path on the spine of the big spur, at about 1400m. Continue now climbing steadily WSW to the Bernhardsegg (or 'eck') guest-house at 1802m. Return by the same route. (1987)

8. SIMMS HUT (2002m)

See Walk 1, possible alternative to the Theodor Haas Way. The routes from the Simms Hut to the Kaiserjochhaus and to the Ansbacher Hut are both serious.

To visit the Simms Hut from the Lech Valley start from Sulzelbach, 6 or 7km up the valley from Elbigenalp. A notice tells you that the path to the Sulzel Alm, the Ronig Alm and the Simms Hut goes 'durch Tunnel' (through tunnels), and a glance at the cliffs to the east reveals the entrances (or exits) to these. The path (636) actually a drivable, though private road at first, climbs through forest until suddenly and dramatically it breaks out on to the rugged cliff face through whose buttresses many tunnels (we lost count) of varying length have been driven. They are roughly made and wet. Often the exit is not visible from the entrance. Between them, and through one great jagged 'window', the views down the valley are impressive. Before the tunnels were made the Sulzeltal must have been a veritable 'Lost Valley' reached only by an obscure and difficult track. Now it is easy going with the Simms Hut in sight from an early stage. The hut is finally reached by steep zig-zags. Frederic Simms was evidently one of those British Alpinists who opened up the Austrian mountains. A photograph at the hut describes him as 'of London' and gives him a qualification in engineering.

Return by the same route. (1987)

9. VENETBERG (2513m) See map p39

A cuckoo in this nest! From the Lechtal high-level paths, and especially when descending from the Steinsee Hut you will have seen the Venetberg to the south-east. Although this mountain belongs officially to the Otztal Group, being a northern outlier of the Kaunergrat on the west side of the Pitztal, it seems more useful to place it here, as it is easily accessible from Imst (train to Zams) and gives the finest of all panoramic views of the Lechtal Alps.

Take the Venetberg cable-car from Zams (775m) to Krahberg (2208m). A chair-lift to the summit has long been planned and may by now exist; in any case it is an easy walk now to the summit (2513m) about 300m higher. It is delightful to walk along the broad 'ridge' to the NE, picking out the now familiar features of the Lechtal Alps to the NW. If you are tempted to go on losing height as far as the Venet Alm at 1918m, you will find that this has been reached by cars. If you

III: THE LECHTAL ALPS WALK 8

SULZELBACH

Tunnels

Sulzenbach

SULZEL ALM

RONIG ALM

SIMMS HUT

can hitch a lift to the valley - do so! To descend to Imsterau involves over 1000m of unpleasant, endlessly long, winding forestry roads. After 7hrs from the Venetberg summit we were fortunately picked up by a forestry VW - you might not be so lucky! Be warned!

(1975)

IV: The Karwendel
(AVE Group 5)

The Name: The eponymous hero of the Karwendel (the legendary character from whom its name is supposed to be derived) is said to be a medieval huntsman called 'Gerwentil'.

Boundaries of the Group: The R. Isar from Scharnitz on the Austro-German frontier to Fall on the Sylvensteinspeicher - Walchen - the Achenbach - the Achensee - the Käsbach - the R. Inn from Jenbach to Zirl (junction with the Niederbach) - the Seefelder Sattel - the Drahnbach - the R. Isar to Scharnitz.

The Karwendel, or Karwendelgebirge, to give the group its full name, is a mountain group clearly defined by the rivers Isar and Inn and their tributaries. To Innsbruck on the Inn, the Karwendel is in effect part of the city, seen through the windows of houses, churches, offices: Innsbruck's own mountains. From Munich on the Isar it is a ragged saw-toothed edge on the horizon in good weather and today a mere hour's drive away. It consists primarily of four great limestone mountain chains (Ketten) lying west-east: the Northern Karwendel Chain, including the Ostl. Karwendelspitze (2537m); the Hinterautal Chain with the Birkkarspitze (2749m); the Gleiersch Chain, with the Bettelwurf (2649m) and the Southern Karwendel Chain, also confusingly called the Nordkette (North Chain) because this is how it appears to the inhabitants of Innsbruck. The great chains have branches, and in the NW the Soiern Spitze (2259m) is the highest point of a quite separate group. Most of the Karwendel is in Austria, but the Soiern Group is entirely in Bavaria. Walks 1, 2, 3, & 7 are entirely in Germany, though Austrian in character.

Parallel with the mountain chains and lying between them run great west-east valleys, and the crossing of the whole area from Scharnitz to Pertisau through the valleys is a favourite expedition.

British visitors driving from the north will find accommodation in or near Mittenwald, and there is an excellent (not cheap) camping site, Naturcamping Isarhorn, in natural, wooded surroundings at a great bend in the R. Isar between Krün and Mittenwald. (You will get accustomed to the military shooting-range nearby!)

IV: KARWENDEL

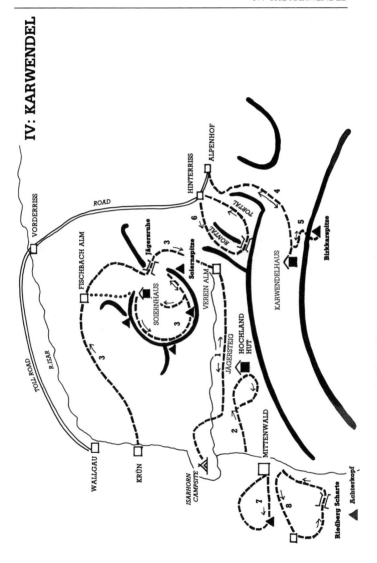

1. THE JÄGERSTEIG (The Hunter's Path)

An exploratory valley walk from the Isarhorn Campsite (bus stop also).
Cross the main road from the campsite and take a track on the north side of the Seinsbach (a tributary that joins the Isar here). This climbs steeply to avoid the Seinsbachklamm, a gorge; then crosses the river and goes up to the Aschauer Alm; refreshments and open views to the west. Above this begins the Jägersteig, a fine path leading up the steep-sided valley and crossing several steep water courses. Across the valley are the southern flanks of the Soiern Group (Walk 3). $2^{1}/_{2}$hrs easy going brings you to the Ferein (or Verein) Alm (1410m) (refreshments), where there is also an unwardened AV hut, the Krinner-Kofler Hut (Cat. I). Return the same way, or less pleasantly by road on the north side of valley. (See also Walk 3.)   (1982)

2. HOCHLAND HUT (1630m Cat. I)

A walk on the edge of the group.
The start of the path up the valley of the Gassellahnbach is tricky to find because of barracks and the Mittenwald by-pass. It is on the east side of the Isar valley about half-way between Isarhorn and Mittenwald. If you have a car drive to the spot, just east of the barracks, using the map. Reasonable parking. Rather over a kilometre up the Gassellahnbach valley there is a sign warning you to take an alternative route if the path is underwater: obviously it often is! For the alternative, turn right, cross the stream and walk up to the Untere Kälberalm. Left here, up, then down, then up very long and steeply to the Obere Kälberalm (apparently private holiday accommodation) then up a pleasant ridge to the Hochland Hut. There is only limited catering at this hut, but the food and welcome are both warm.

(The 'wet' route continues up the Gassellahnbach, forking right at a river-fork and later winding its way up to the Obere Kälberalm from the north.)

Continue from the hut on a high traversing path, south, then gradually west, on the north slopes of the Predigtstuhl (1920m) until you reach a 'cross-road' below the Dammkar Hut (1650m privately owned) and above the Untere Kälberalm. Turn right and drop steeply down past this to join your original route home.

(1982)

3. THE SOIERNHAUS (1616m. Cat. I) AND
THE SOIERN 'HORSESHOE'.

The Soiern group is virtually an independent massif, divided from the main Karwendel chains by the Seinsbach and Fermebach valleys.

By bus to Krün: this allows you to return by a different route. East of the village a forest road rises and gradually swings round to the SE to the Fischbach Alm (1403m) ($1^{3/4}$hrs). From here a choice: either on the *Lakeiensteig* on the west of the valley, with some tricky places but no loss of height, or down by the road to the so-called Hundestall, a pleasant valley pasture, then up through open woodland leading to an excellently engineered wide zig-zag path up to the hut, marvellously situated on the very rim of the Soiernkessel, a lovely basin wholly surrounded by mountains and adorned with lakes, worth walking down to.

The hut was built for the tragic 'fairy-tale' King of Bavaria, Wagner's patron, Ludwig II, as a royal hunting lodge in 1866, and the excellent path was doubtless made for his use. How seriously we must take the name of the more difficult route, *Lakeiensteig* (the Lackeys' Path), remains uncertain. The hut was taken over in 1921, three years after the abdication of the last king of Bavaria, and enlarged in 1968. The wardens in 1982 had been every summer for 29 years, but intended to give up after 30.

The round walk of the Soiern Ridge is deservedly popular and is best done anti-clockwise. Follow Ludwig's *Reitsteig* (bridle path) due west from the hut and the first summit, the Schöttelkarspitze (2050m) is reached without difficulty in a little over an hour: a sudden and amazing view to Mittenwald and beyond. The ridge ahead looks slightly like the Snowdon Horseshoe. You must retreat a few yards from the precipitous south side of the summit and go round, moving on to mild scrambling almost to the summit of the Feldernkreuz (2048m). Look back as you go: it seems impossible you have been on the summit of the Schöttelkarspitze! Easy going after this to the Feldernkopf (2071m) and thence across the Soiern Schneid at the head of a really vast gully, the Reissende Lahn, that splits the massif from top to bottom - about 600m. You can see down it to the Ferein Alm and Jägersteig (Walk 1). Stupendous views all the way to Mittenwald, into Austria, and of innumerable mountains, including the Zugspitze.

Schöttelkarspitze

Next is the Reissende-Lahn-Spitze (2209m); then down to the Soiernscharte from which the top of the Soiernspitze (2259m) is reached without difficulty (about $2^{1/2}$hrs from the Schöttelkarspitze). From here you can survey all the northern cliffs and tops of the Karwendel, whilst due north lie the Walchensee and the Kochelsee. This is the day's goal: make the most of it.

Now you must return to the Soiernscharte and go down into the Soiernkessel, steep scree at first and quite a scramble lower down to between the twin lakes; and so up to the hut.

To vary the return walk from the hut and to make a round walk of the whole, do not go back to the Fischbach Alm by either route, but take a rising path SE within the Soiern Basin to the eastern col of the rim, Jägersruh (Hunter's Rest): you can look back at the hut for a long time. On the far side of the Jägersruh (new aspect of the Soiernspitze) follow, after the initial drop, an almost level cattle track that eventually reaches the Jöchl (little pass) near Hirzeneck (1801m).

(From here there is also a direct path from the Soiernspitze summit.)

It is worth leaving the path to make the most of Hirzeneck as a viewpoint. Now you have to drop 400m to the Ferein Alm (refreshments) .

Return via the Jägersteig (Walk 1). You will now appreciate the Reissende-Lahn and enjoy picking out the Feldernkreuz.

4. THE KARWENDELHAUS (1765m Cat. I)

Walkers doing the Great Karwendel Crossing, west to east, approach this hut from Scharnitz - some 15km of drivable road (not public); there is even a taxi from Scharnitz to the hut! The route from Hinterriss described here is shorter and more interesting and varied

From Wallgau, about 10km north of Mittenwald drive east along a beautiful toll road through the Isar valley north of the Soiern group. At Vorderriss you turn south on a public road up the Risstal. This road crosses the frontier more than once before reaching Hinterriss, where there is a customs post. *Have your passport with you.* Drive a little further to the Alpenhof guest-house (945m): large car park. Cross the road. A sign directs you almost due south across meadows, over the river, and steeply up through woods to join Path 231 from Hinterriss. (Older guidebooks and maps are misleading, as a forestry road has forced changes.) Follow this south-east at first, then swinging south round a broad spur of Luchsegg (1308m) into the Johannis Tal: a fine view up to the Karwendel cliffs at the head of the valley, with the river far below and to your left. The path is quite exciting, as it has to cross several steep gullies; then it drops down to the forestry road, but be alert for waymarks. You need walk very little on the road. The path runs parallel *below* it for a time, rejoins it, and does *not* drop to the valley-bottom when the road does, but keeps its height, climbing for a time in steep curves until you reach the K1. Ahorn Boden - open pastures with scattered groups of trees dominated on the south side by the cliffs of the central Karwendel range. Do not leave this area without paying due homage to Hermann von Barth, who opened up the area to mountaineers. His memorial is near the path.

From the K1. Ahorn Boden the track climbs in great curves from 1403m in the Boden to 1803m at the Hochalmsattel: east-west watershed. Glorious scenery all the way. From the saddle gently down about 1km to the Karwendelhaus (1765m) on its dramatic spur at the head of the Karwendel Tal. (4hrs from Alpenhof.) A grand hut in every respect.   (1982)

5.   THE BIRKKARSPITZE (2749m)

This is the highest summit in the Karwendel, but is quite easily accessible to surefooted walkers, and very rewarding.

From the Karwendelhaus just a few yards to the east along the Hochalmsattel path and there is a sign to the right where the route to the Birkkarspitze begins with fixed ropes up and across rocks whose wetness is probably permanent. This slightly intimidating prelude is soon over, however, and you round a corner on a good path south into a huge corrie, the Schlauchkar.

(About $^{1}/_{2}$hr from the hut a path left that climbs in steep zig-zags to the summit of the Hochalmkreuz (2192m. 1hr) - recommended as a soft option instead of the Birkkarspitze in uncertain weather or with children.)

From the Hochalmkreuz junction the Birkkarspitze route climbs, often with steep zig-zags on often unstable scree all the way to the Schlauchkar Sattel (2635m) where the little Birkkar Hut is tucked away among the rocks. Do not be misled by the optimistic 'bed' symbol in the AV Green Hut Book! The hut is a mere shed with fixed benches; but a welcome refuge, and doubtless a life-saver on occasion. You could leave your rucksack here.

Go east from the hut for the summit, about 100m higher up. It is reached on good rock by pleasant scrambling protected by fixed ropes. Cross, book and magnificent views in all directions. (2$^{1}/_{2}$hrs from Karwendelhaus.) Then down the protected scramble to the little hut again.

(West from the Schlauchkar Sattel lies the 3-topped ridge mountain, the Ödkarspitzen (2743m). This can be reached by the surefooted on a well-marked route, protected by fixed ropes in exposed places. The traverse of the three tops is similar, but involves one 3m. rock step. There is an alternative return route, the Brendelsteig, of similar standard, that goes down from the Western Summit of the Ödkarspitzen (careful route finding necessary!) and joins the Schlauchkar path just above the Hochalmkreuz junction.)

From the Schlauchkar Sattel return down the Schlauchkar where good scree-runners have a great advantage: you can make it from the Birkkar Hut (2635m) to the Karwendelhaus (1765m) - 870m of descent - in 1$^{1}/_{4}$hrs. (1982)

6. RONTAL-TORTAL: THE TWO-VALLEYS WALK

Don't be misled by the description of this as the finest valley walk in the whole area: it involves an ascent of 884m, so is quite a mountain day.

Drive to Hinterriss (see Walk 4) and park there. (Do not drive on to Alpenhof.) Walk up the Rontal (or Rohntal) NW, then SW, up a good forestry road. Views north to the Schafreuter (2100m) with the Tölzer Hut (1835m) below its summit. This road goes as far as the Rontal Alm at 1262m, set in open pastures with the magnificent precipices of the Eastern Karwendel Spitze (2537m) due south. Walk towards this, climbing ever more steeply, finally turning east and climbing the last 250m or so in very steep zig-zags to the Torscharte (1815m). Wonderful viewpoint, including the whole Soiern Group (Walk 3) to the NW.

The descent through the Tortal is scenically far superior even to the Rontal. Picturesquely past the Tortal Hochleger (1592m), a primitive alm hut inhabited in summer, then steeply down to the Tortal Niederleger (1144m), followed by the 2$^{1}/_{2}$km walk almost due north down the beautiful Tortal to Hinterriss. A walk not to be missed; but choose good weather for the scenic rewards. (1982)

7. HOHER KRANZBERG (1397m)
(An additional walk from Mittenwald.)

This walk and the next do not actually belong to the Karwendel but lie west of the Isar on the edge of the Wettersteingebirge and Mieminger Kette (AVE Group 4). But they are pleasant off-day outings from Mittenwald. Starting from the church in Mittenwald, scorn the chair-lift and walk up the signed path past the Kalvarienberg and you will reach the top (refreshment house just below it, if open) in about 1³/₄hrs. Then follow paths to the Wildensee, NE of the Kranzberg, with a good refreshment house. Then direct from here back to Mittenwald, through pleasant country, but the route is rather 'roady'.

8. LEUTASCH KLAMM AND RIEDBERGSCHARTE (1454m)
(An additional walk from Mittenwald. See Walk 7)

The Leutasch Klamm (river-filled gorge) just south of Mittenwald, is short but impressive and is allegedly the first 'klamm' ever to be made accessible to the public. The old wooden gangways having been swept away by phenomenally high water in the 1970s, new, steel-strutted gangways have been built by the local brewery.

Having made certain that you are carrying your passport, follow forest paths south, towards the Grosse Arnspitze (2196m) but quite soon - less than 1km - branch right (west) through woods on the northern slopes of the Schartenkopf (1610m). You will have the curious experience of crossing a national frontier (big notices) on a stroll through woods. The path, now in Austria, eventually brings you out on the Mittenwald-Telfs road near a customs post (Zollamt) at Schanz. Go through this and you will soon reach Burggraben with its excellent hostelry, the *Mühle*. What better place for a leisurely meal! From the Mühle walk SE, climbing about 400m to the Riedbergscharte (1454m), on the frontier (big notices), on a well wooded ridge, with a well-sited hunting lodge, and quite good views east.

(To the right, SW is the way to the Gr. Arnspitze (2196m), described as being not easy and only for the experienced.)

For the present walk, turn left, NE and walk back to the 'Klamm'. The path is obvious, steep in places but pleasant, on wooded slopes.

(1982)

V: The Kaisergebirge
(AVE Group 8)

The Name: The name, 'The Emperor's Mountains' is some 750 years old and is first used in a Bavarian Ducal Inventory of the 13th century. The form 'Wilder Kaiser' first appears in 1611 -'Wild' having the primary sense of English 'wild' and not, as in the high alpine regions of Austria, 'snow-covered'. The term *Zahmer (Tame) Kaiser* for the northern range is comparatively modern and was first introduced in 1870 by a certain Thomas Trautwein to avoid the confusions arising from the older 'Vorder-' and 'Hinter-' (Front- and Back-) whose application obviously varied according to one's topographical viewpoint.

Boundaries of the Group: The junction of the Jenn with the Inn (about 6km N of Kufstein) - the Jenn - the Achentaler Bach - Durchholzen - Walchsee - the Weisenbach -the Kössener Ache (Grosse Ache) as far as St. Johann-im-Tirol - Reitner Ache - Ellmau - the Weissache - the Glemmache - the Inn to the junction with the Jenn.

The Kaisergebirge is usually thought of, in this country at least, as being the preserve of the hard rock-climber, where 'Fleischbank' and 'Totenkirchl' are names to conjure with; but it also offers walks of every standard - rambles amid romantically savage, almost theatrical scenery, high-level paths, 2000m summits and protected routes on climbers' terrain.

Kufstein is the obvious base town from which to explore the group. It is on the Munich-Innsbruck motorway and has accommodation, and an excellent campsite behind the *Bären* guest-house at the south end of the town. The town, strategically placed, has been of great importance in military history and is dominated by a grim and impressive 'Festung' (fortress). This houses a colossal open-air organ, the *Heldenorgel* (Organ of the Heroes), which is played from a console in a courtyard and whose glorious sound comes from one of the towers of the fortress and can be heard for miles around. It is a memorial to the fallen of both World Wars, and

V: KAISERGEBIRGE

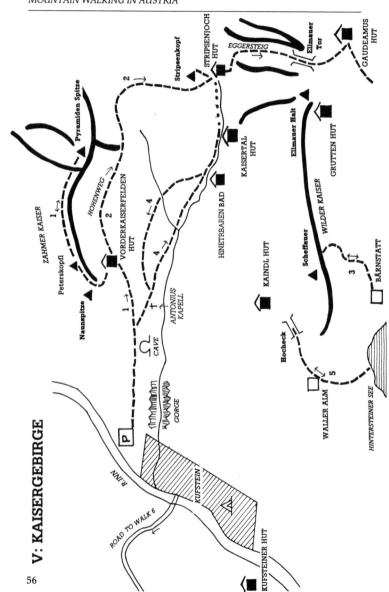

I doubt whether anyone, whatever their nationality or political persuasion, can fail to be moved when *Ich hatt' einen Kameraden* is played on it, with glockenspiel.

The Kaisergebirge is like a vast letter H lying on its side from west to east. The southern limb is the rocky Wilder Kaiser and the northern the Zahmer Kaiser. A green crossbar of hills and alms joins these and divides the western valley, the Kaisertal, from the eastern, the Kaiserbachtal. The Stripsenjoch (1580m) with the imposing Stripsenjochhaus - it sleeps over 200 - lies on the crossbar at the centre of all.

1. THE ZAHMER KAISER: THE VORDERKAISERFELDEN HUT (1384m Cat. I) AND THE PYRAMIDEN SPITZE (1999m)

A scenically rewarding walk and a good introduction to the group.

Pleasantly across flat meadows to the NE of the town, passing the Loretto Chapel, to Sparchen. The path into the Kaisertal starts at Sparchenmühle (mill) just N of the Kaiserbach (Sparchen Bach). There is also a large car park and bus stop here. The wide, partly stepped, steep and winding 'mule-track' is, because of the gorge, the Kienbergklamm, through which the river emerges, the only way into the valley, and the jeeps and Nevas you will see in the Kaisertal have all had to be winched up this path in the first instance. The initial climb over, follow the track past Rupp (Ruepp) and Zottenhof to the Veitenhof guest-house (35mins from car park). Between Rupp and Zottenhof you will see the signpost to the Tischoferhöhle (cave) but will probably leave this for another occasion (see Walk 4). About 10mins beyond Veitenhof the route - still suitable for jeeps - branches left (No. 816) for the Pfandl Alm, Riez Alm and the Vorderkaiserfelden Hut: from Veitenhof almost a full 700m of ascent.

The old, large, rambling and friendly hut, which is open all the year round, this being ski-country, has a fine situation with spacious views of the Kaisertal, the north face of the Wilder Kaiser, and the Inn valley with the Rofangebirge on its far side. Evening light on the Wilder Kaiser and mornings when the mist-filled Inn valley resembles a mighty glacier are memorable experiences.

The route (816) to the Pyramiden Spitze begins by climbing steeply up the extreme western end of the Zahmer Kaiser, soon reaching a saddle. To your left is the Naunspitze (1635m), a steep rocky pyramid reached without difficulty by a diversion of about 10mins. It is the most westerly 'top' of the Zahmer Kaiser, with outstanding views of the Inn Valley and the Wilder Kaiser. About this point you will realise that the 'Tame Kaiser' is tame only on its southern slopes: to the north it is impressively precipitous. Whether or not you visit the Naunspitze, turn sharp R here and follow the marked path to the summit of the Peterskopfl (1746m). Now follow waymarks easily along the latschen-covered, rocky and picturesque plateau passing by the Einserkogel (1925m) and the Zwölferkogel (1912m). (Names like Elfer-Zwölfer- or Einser-kogel are based on the position of the sun at the hours of 11, 12, 1 etc.) The only striking feature of the route occurs at this point - the Vogelbadkamin (Bird-bath Chimney) - a very easy chimney-like gully, which must now be descended. (It takes its name from a nearby spring.) Then a wide bend to the N leads over the Elferkogel (1916m), and so SE to the summit of the Pyramiden Spitze (1999m), a great viewpoint and the highest named summit in the Zahmer Kaiser. (There is an unnamed point 2.7m higher, a little to the south of it!) Return same route, pausing to admire the northern profile of the Einserkogel before scrambling up the Vogelbadkamin. ($2^{1/2}$hrs, hut-Pyramiden Spitze.) (1980)

2. THE EGGERSTEIG AND THE ELLMAUER TOR

(Vorderkaiserfelden Hut (1384m. Cat. I) - Hohenweg - Stripsenjoch Haus (1580m. Cat. I) - Eggersteig - Steinerne Rinne - Ellmauer Tor (1995m) - Gaudeamus Hut (1267m. Cat. I) - Ellmau.)

The walk described here is perhaps the most ambitious open to walkers in this area. The Eggersteig is one of the oldest of the kind of protected rock routes now dubbed Via Ferrata (Iron Way), and was established in 1903. It demands mountaineering experience and freedom from giddiness, and becomes dangerous (NOT merely 'difficult') when wet, snowy or icy.

For the approach to the Vorderkaiserfelden Hut, see Walk 1. The Hohenweg starts SE from the hut and traverses the southern side of the Zahmer Kaiser as high as possible without encountering its crags and steep corries: do not take any branches up or down. At one point you will cross the path that leads directly up to the Pyramiden Spitze from Bärenbad. The route is a sun-trap but with incomparable views into the Kaisertal and across to the Wilder Kaiser, which is visible from the Scheffauer (2113m, see Walk 3) in the west, to the Ellmauer Halt (2394m) and beyond towards the east. In 2hrs or so you reach the Hochalm (1410m), a 'dream-alm' lying on the crossbar of the H. Then walk south along the 'crossbar', which is very green and picturesque against the rocky backdrop, with a good deal of down and up, until, having skirted the Stripsenkopf (1809m) on its western slopes, you arrive at the rather white and obtrusive Stripsenjoch Haus. (About 1³/₄hrs from the Hochalm.)

If you have enjoyed solitude until now, it ends here, for 600m below at the Griesner Alm at the head of the Kaiserbach Tal is a huge car park, a desecration to walkers but a boon to rock-climbers with heavy loads of ironmongery who make this hut their base for the famous Wilder Kaiser rock routes. This hut can also be reached on foot through the Kaisertal (see Walk 4).

For escape from the crowds and for the views the Stripsenkopf is worth a visit during the afternoon, and if the weather is favourable the Stripsenjoch Hut sees beautiful evenings and sunsets.

The next day, given favourable weather, you climb the Eggersteig to the Ellmauer Tor.

Start with a zig-zag descent on the east side of the joch into the Wildanger, a basin or corrie lying between the feet of the Totenkirchl and the Fleischbank. After the last zig-zag the path to the valley continues straight on but we take a little path to the right that traverses in a curve around the corrie and leads to the first protected section of the Eggersteig, an exposed, dramatically airy up-and-down traverse of the north cliffs of the Fleischbank.

This leads to the Steinerne Rinne (Stone Groove) a vast slabby gully, improbably steep (for walkers!), hemmed in by the precipices of the Fleischbank and the Predigtstuhl. The route is hugely impressive, but well protected by fixed ropes. Beware of stones dislodged by careless persons higher up!

The upper part is wider and less steep, more like a corrie, and leads easily up scree and snow to the Ellmauer Tor (1995m). When you reach this you realise that it justifies its name, The Ellmau Gate, for it is indeed a titanic gate through the mountain range. It takes its name from Ellmau, the little town to the south from which it is clearly seen. From the Tor you have an entirely new view: the

Eastern Alps, dominated by the Grosser Venediger.

(From here there is a popular ascent - 35mins, Grade I - to the Hintere Goinger Halt, 2195m. Allow time for this if you want to include it.)

From the Stripsenjoch to the Ellmauer Tor will have taken $2^{1/4}$-$2^{1/2}$hrs. The descent on the south side is easier, but not without interest: at first over snow and scree into the Kübelkar and over to its right side, where there is a rock section with fixed ropes. Finally down latschen-covered slopes and scattered beech woods to the happily named Gaudeamus ('Let-us-rejoice') Hut (1267m Cat. I).

It is a dull trudge down to Ellmau, so if you can get a jeep lift - even if squashed in with children and dogs - don't refuse it! There is a good bus service from Ellmau back to Kufstein. (Time-table in hut.)   (1980)

3. THE SCHEFFAUER (2113m)

The Scheffauer is the most westerly summit of the Wilder Kaiser. The easiest ascent - that from the south - is described here.

Drive - or walk if necessary - from Scheffau, the village from which the mountain takes its name, to Bärnstatt, a tiny settlement with a red-roofed, red-turreted little church. You can already see the summit from here and it is by the church that you start. The path climbs pleasantly - but don't lose it! - through woods. You pass a ruined alm and zig-zag up to a grassy saddle. Left here, and soon right, up a miniature valley to the Steiner-Hochalm (1257m). Up grass, north, from here and through woods and right to a big scree-field (unpleasant in descent). Above the scree bear left on to a good, rocky rising traverse path leading to the Hochofen, a sort of shallow cave with an awkwardly high fixed rope as help up a bit of slab. Then round to the right to unexpectedly dramatic scenery, the path coming up between a rock tower and the main mass of the mountain. Continue up until you reach the saddle between the Scheffauer and the Westlicher Hackenkopf. Here the route from the north, the Wildauersteig, comes up. Turn left and 10 easy minutes bring you to the summit with its cross and book. The panorama is tremendous, but most exciting is the view to the NE and E along the massively architectured 'ridge' of the Wilder Kaiser to the Ellmauer Halt.

Return same way. Take particular care at the Hochofen: it is the German for 'blast-furnace', by the way; and enjoy the view of the

Hintersteiner See from the Steiner-Hochalm. (Time for ascent $3^{1}/_{2}$-4hrs.) (1980)

4. THE KAISERTAL

This walk is scenically very rewarding but can be extremely hot.

Enter the Kaisertal as on Walk 1, but do not fork left for the Vorderkaiserfelden Hut. Continue instead, past the Pfandlhof Guesthouse to the Antonius Kapelle - a popular picture. Go on past this, leaving Hinterkaiserhof on your right, and continue further, losing height a little, until you get to Hinterbärenbad, where you will find the Anton-Karg-Haus (831m. Cat. I).

(Alternatively, soon after the Pfandlhof, a forestry road runs below this old route, almost level, with two tunnels. It joins the old route at Triftklause and is about $^{1}/_{2}$hr shorter.)

From Hinterbärenbad continue, passing a picturesque but sad group of memorials to climbers, for about 20mins to the Kaisertal Haus (Hans-Berger Haus) (936m), a hut of the Naturfreunde (Friends of Nature). As so often with Naturfreunde huts it is friendly and has an informal atmosphere. This is our goal for today.

(Behind this hut the path soon begins its long, steep climb of over 600m to the Stripsenjoch Haus.)

To vary the return and gain more extensive views, take a path to the right (NW) at Bärenbad. This crosses the Bärental and rejoins our original route near the Antonius Kapelle. It is picturesque, especially in its early part, but much of it has been made into a bare, drivable road. From the Antonius Kapelle return by original route.

While in the Kaisertal it is worthwhile visiting the Tischoferhöhle: sign and path a little W of Zottenhof. It is only 8mins to the cave but easy to miss the turn and to continue all the way down into the 'Klamm'. This is indeed worth a visit, but the trip will take longer. The cave is of great archaeological interest. The bones of some 300 cave-bears and other animals were found there and traces of human habitation from Neolithic times, 4,000 years old. (See the museum in the Kufstein Fortress.) (1980)

5. THE WALLER ALM AND HOCHECK (1470m)

This little walk completes your broad exploration of the Kaisergebirge from Kufstein without either having recourse to a cable-car or actually entering the area served by the Kaiserlift and Wilder Kaiser chair-lift.

Drive or walk through Scheffau beyond Bärnstatt to the Hintersteiner See (good bathing place) and follow marked paths to the Waller Alm (1171m), a dairy-farm and guest-house open all the year round, whose proprietor has (or had) a gift for doggerel, lettering and woodwork, resulting in a series of delightful signboards. It is set in pleasantly hummocky country formed during the Ice Ages. Continue above it, NE, then E and finally NE again to Hocheck - a grassy saddle.

From here you can not only see the whole south face of the Zahmer Kaiser, much of the north face of the Wilder Kaiser and much of the Inn Valley, but also the large winter-skiing area around the Kaindl Hut (1318m privately owned), which has been invisible from all the other walks described.

(Of course the Hocheck can also be reached from the Kaindl Hut.) (1980)

6. PENDLING (1563m) AND THE HÖHLENSTEIN HUT.

(An additional walk from Kufstein.) This walk does not actually belong to the Kaisergebirge but is on the edge of the Rofangebirge on the NW side of the Inn. However, it is a walk to be undertaken from Kufstein, and Pendling itself, with the Kufsteiner Haus (1562m) (privately owned) almost at its summit, is a dominant feature of the Kufstein skyline.

Cross the Inn in Kufstein and drive up the steep road from Morsbach, past the Thier See and south on a side road to Schneeberg (guesthouse). Limited parking. From here a good path leads to the summit of Pendling (1563m) and a little NE of this to the Kufsteiner Haus on the tip of the ridge with magnificent views of the Kufstein and the Kaisergebirge.

After due refreshment walk SW along the ridge over Pendling and the Mittagkopf, dropping down to the little Kaler Alm (not a refreshment house) and after further walk in the same general direction, to the Höhlenstein Hut (1259m) a good refreshment house set in a broad, grassy basin. From here, tracks and forest paths back to Schneeberg. (1980)

VI: The Berchtesgaden Alps
(AVE Group 10)

The Name: The name of the group, which, of course is that of the German town at its centre, may be derived from a medieval male forename *Perther* and the word *Gaden,* a single-storey house, perhaps a hunting-lodge. So the name probably means, *Perther's Hunting-Lodge.*

Boundaries of the Group: The R. Salzach from Salzburg to Bischofshofen - Mühlbach - Trockenbach - the Dientner Sattel - the Filzensattel - Hintertal - Urslau - the R. Saalach to Salzburg.

As a glance at the map will show, almost the whole length of the boundary of this group is in Austria, but within it lies a great equilateral triangle of Germany, with each side some 25km long and its apex to the south connected with the rest of Germany only by an 'isthmus' a mere 11km wide. At the heart of the group stands the German town of Berchtesgaden. This popular resort, with an excellent, though sloping, campsite, is the base for the walks described. Thus at Berchtesgaden we are geographically *within Austria,* though not politically.

The map also shows that this apparent intrusion of Germany into Austria is historically and politically not as absurd as it at first appears, for Berchtesgaden is protected from Austria by a horseshoe of high mountains with its open side to the north.

In the second half of the 20th century the name 'Berchtesgaden' is inextricably linked with that of Germany's evil Austrian, dictator, Adolf Hitler, who had his *Eagle's Nest* on the Kehlstein (1837m) south-east of the town. On the site of the Nazi chief's eyrie the Americans, with questionable taste, have built their General Walker Hotel for US Forces. There is no need to visit this particular 'tourist attraction'.

The area between a line roughly from Ramsau to the Hoher Göll, and the state frontier is a national park. This includes the Watzmann massif and the Königssee.

Of the many shorter walks at lower levels near Berchtesgaden

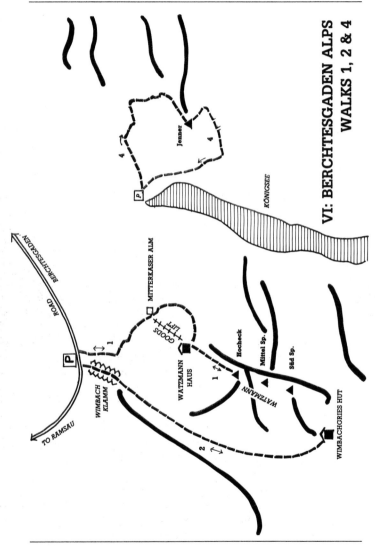

VI: BERCHTESGADEN ALPS
WALKS 1, 2 & 4

Hintersee from Kridlonscharte

Elmsee and Pühringer Hut, Totesgebirge
East from Tamischbachturm, Ennstaler Alps

the most interesting (though it does not qualify for description as a mountain walk) is through the Almbachklamm. This amazing 3km gorge was opened up in 1894, with 320 steps, a tunnel, 29 bridges and 168m of path carved out of the rock. At its lower, eastern end, about half-way between Berchtesgaden and Marktschellenberg, is a cannon-ball mill (Kugelmühle), an ingeniously simple device by which the stream rolls stones in a circular groove until they are spherical. No longer used as cannon-balls, they are now sold to tourists. You can make a round walk of this by heading north out of Berchtesgaden to Hintergern and Dürrlehen, then down to the Theresienklause (dam, built 1836). Then downstream through the ever increasingly narrow and thrilling Klamm via the gangways, bridges and niches, with waterfalls galore until you reach the Kugelmühle. From here a path on the west side of the Berchtesgadener Ache takes you back to Berchtesgaden without having to walk on the road.

1. THE WATZMANN

(The Watzmann Haus (1914m Cat. I) and the Watzmann-Hocheck (2651m).)

Park at the foot of the Wimbachtal on the road from Berchtesgaden to Ramsau. Do not go into the Wimbachklamm (see Walk 2) but take a path climbing pleasantly through woods, which soon joins a track leading past the Stuben Alm to the Mitterkaser Alm, where refreshment is available - at least beer or milk. The goods cable-way to the Watzmann Haus starts near here.

This is the end of the track. The path goes up SSW to the ruined Falz-Alm, and then more steeply, west, with many zig-zags to the imposing hut (4hrs). Fine views on the way, especially of the Kleiner (Little) Watzmann and the Watzmannkinder (Watzmann-children), all repeating their father's distinctive shape on a smaller scale.

The ascent of the Watzmann-Hocheck, 2651m, the most northerly of the mountain's three summits, is rough and stony, with a couple of fixed ropes but no problems (2hrs). Steep cliffs to the left with perilous cornices when there is snow. Fantastic views in all directions, from the Zugspitze to the Dachstein. This summit has a small cross, a ruined wooden hut among the rocks and an equally ruined 'long-drop' loo on a cliff-edge.

To the south the Cuillin-like ridge leads to the Mittelspitze (2713m), the highest point in the Berchtesgaden Alps.

(This ridge is very narrow in places and is furnished here and there with wire ropes and artificially cut steps. Very few of the walkers who reach the Hocheck seem to continue. *This* solitary walker decided at all events that it was 'sound mountaineering judgement', being alone, to give up at the narrowest point: it felt very lonely! But there appeared to be no real problems for any experienced party.)

Return to the Watzmann Haus by the same route, say 1¹/₂ hrs.

(The Watzmann Haus can also be approached from Ilsank or Königssee. The complete traverse of the three summits leads to a difficult, unwaymarked descent at the southern end. Not recommended except to experienced mountaineers.)   (1979)

2. WIMBACHKLAMM AND WIMBACHTAL

This is a valley walk of curious character and with some spectacular mountain scenery. It reaches 1327m.

Park as for Walk 1, but this time pay the modest fee to enter the Wimbachklamm (it is a 'return ticket', by the way). The Klamm is only about 300yds long, but very beautiful and dramatic, with veil-like waterfalls streaming down its side. As usual in such places, you walk safely on wooden gangways.

Above the Klamm the valley is picturesque at first, and after about an hour you reach the Wimbachschloss, a former hunting-lodge. Above this the valley widens into a great stony wilderness with a strange, almost solemn atmosphere. This was once a lake like the Königssee but is now filled with giant rivers of stones, through which flow the mountain streams. The weird barrenness of the valley floor is compensated for by the rugged rock mountains on both sides and the increasingly majestic rock scenery. Another 2hrs brings you to the Wimbachgries Hut (1327m. Naturfreunde), refreshments and accommodation.

(This is the terminus for the - mountaineering - traverse of the Watzmann; interesting paths above the hut lead over spiky mountains.)

Enjoy the walk back down the valley and see the Klamm in afternoon light.   (1979)

3. THE SCHELLENBERG ICE-CAVE (1570m)

A cave can legitimately be the object of a mountain walk when its entrance is at 1570m only about 300m below the summit ridge of the Untersberg, the mountain that links Salzburg and Berchtesgaden, its northern summit being the Salzburger Hochthron (1853m) and its southern the Berchtesgadener Hochthron (1972m). This is the largest ice-cave in Germany open to the public, and, weather permitting, is open from mid-May until October. It is a genuine ice-cave, summer temperature between -0.5° and +1.0°C- So carry something warm, even in hot weather.

From Berchtesgaden drive to Marktschellenberg and park near the Old Customs Tower (Mautturm) just north of the village and about 1km south of the modern frontier. (Austria is *north* of Germany here!) The path leaves the road on the west side and presents no navigational or other problems (blue / red waymarks). It leads to the Mitterkaser Hunting Lodge in about 1³/₄hrs, after which it steepens and becomes a scenically very beautiful mountain path to the Toni-Lenz Haus (another 1hr beyond the Mitterkaser house), ¹/₄hr from the cave. The entrance to the cave is a wide, fairly low arch, and once inside you immediately encounter ice. The tour is highly organised: every tenth person - if male! - is given an acetylene lamp, and if the tenth person is a woman the guide makes you change places! For spectacular effects the guide uses the old fashioned but exciting method of burning magnesium tape. These effects include an ice

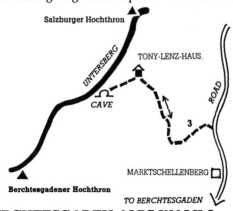

VI: BERCHTESGADEN ALPS WALK 3

'cathedral', complete with altar, pulpit and confessional. This is called the Mörkdom (Mörk Cathedral) in honour of Alexander von Mörk who first reached this point in October 1910.

Return to Marktschellenberg by the same route.   (1979)

4. JENNER (1874m)

This mountain, popular all the year round (for it is an international ski-playground in winter) is, because of its situation, one of the best viewpoints in the whole area, but whether it should be recommended as a walk is at least questionable, for the walk up is both laborious and unexciting, while the 2-stage lift takes passengers from the Königssee to the summit in 22mins. However, even if you take the lazy way up, the walk down is splendid. But you must love your fellow-creatures: this is no lonely summit!

To walk up: start from the vast car park at the northern end of the Königsee and walk east past the bottom station of the Jennerseilbahn. The queues will probably decide you to walk (though it handles 800 persons an hour), but remember you are now at 630m and summit is 1876m, a difference of 1246m, a long climb on a hot day. After less than 1km, at a little place called Holz, take a a path to the right. This makes an arc south of the Brandkopf (1156m) until it reaches Vorderbrand (guest-house, refreshments) on a direct motor-road from Berchtesgaden. Then SSE up open country, crossing a road. You may go to the Jennerseilbahn Middle Station, or by-pass it on its left. Do not follow the road! It goes *round* the mountain. Eventually you will reach the Mitterkaser Alm, where you will find crowds of people eating and drinking. Keep to the right, on a real *path* at last and you will reach the summit.

The actual summit is a tiny, dramatic pyramid with a cross and superlative views of the Königssee to the west and south, and of the Kehlstein and Untersberg to the north. A little below the summit is a further railed viewpoint. Also not far below the summit is the top station of the Jennerseilbahn, with more crowds eating and drinking.

From the summit area come down steeply in zig-zags to the Königsberg Alm, then SW on the Bärenwand - a good path - to the Königsbach Alm, where, if you have waited until now, you can eat and drink without being jostled. From here NW, on the road at first but soon branching left and traversing the Rabenwand, a fine path with continuously good views, back to the Königssee car park.(1979)

VII: The Dachstein-Gebirge
(AVE Group 14)

The Name: The full name 'Dachstein-Gebirge' simply means 'Dachstein Mountains', Dachstein being that of the principal mountain in the group, the Hoher Dachstein (2993m). 'Dachstein' is a 'roofing-slab'.

Boundaries of the Group: Russbach - Pass Gschütt - Gosau - the Gosau Bach - Halstätter See - Pöschenhöhe - Bad Aussee - Karnisch Traun - Bad Mitterndorf - Klachau - Grimmingbach - R. Enns to the junction with the Weissenbach - Ramsaubach - Kalte Mandling - Warme Mandling - Marchegg Sattel - Fritzbach - Linbach - Neubach - Lungötz - the Lammer to its junction with the Russbach.

The 'official' AVE Dachstein group covers a big area as far as Grimming (2351m), a wholly detached mountain, in the east. We are concerned only with the actual Hoher Dachstein massif, south and south-west of Halstatt. Within this group two major walks are described, one (based on Halstatt) primarily within the 'Hoher Dachstein Horseshoe', the other 'round the Gosaukamm', the most westerly branch of the massif. Each walk includes a summit as a bonus.

Halstatt, on the western shore of the Halstätter See, is arguably the most beautiful little town in the world. It is famed in the archaeological world as the seat of the 'Halstatt' period of prehistoric culture, well represented in the local museum. The area is also the setting for Adalbert Stifter's celebrated story *Bergkristall.* In the 1960s Halstatt could only be reached from the north (by public transport) by train to the eastern shore of the lake and then by boat across it. Now a good motor-road has been built down the western shore and Halstatt has been furnished with a remarkable and environmentally most effective by-pass through a tunnel in the mountain high *above* the town. The tunnel even has a 'window' with a lay-by, so that one can park and look out inconspicuously over the town and the lake. Halstatt has good accommodation and a comfortable campsite.

If you are motorised, the obvious 'base' for the Gosaukamm walk is the large long-stay car park at the north-west end of the Vorderer Gosausee, reached by a good road which runs south from the Pass Gschütt (964m) on the road running west from Gosaumühle, north of Halstatt on the Halstätter See.

1. WITHIN THE DACHSTEIN HORSESHOE (3 days)

(Halstatt - Wiesberg Haus (1884m Naturfreunde) - Simony Hut (2203m Cat. I) - Gjaid Alm-Schutzhütte or Schilcher-Haus (1739m privately owned) - Taubenkogel (2301m) - The Dachstein Ice-Caves - Obertraun.)

Start walking up on the south side of the Waldbach Valley from Lahn (c.500m), the most southerly bit of Halstatt, where the campsite, 'Camping Höll' is situated. On the way you will pass the Simony

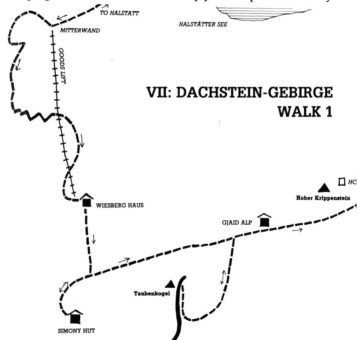

Memorial. Dr. Friedrich Simony was the 19th-century worthy who first explored the Dachstein (see Halstatt Museum). Good views back down to Lahn and the lake. At a spot called Mitterwand is the valley station of the goods cableway to the Wiesberg Haus. You may be able to send your rucksack up if you can operate the telephone. The track continues under cliffs and turns from north-west to south west, overlooking the Waldbach gorge. This is crossed by a dramatic bridge, excellent for photography: but do not cross it. Above the bridge at point 875m, turn sharp left to climb through the woods. Before doing this it is worthwhile going a few yards out of your way to visit the Waldbach Ursprung (913m) where the fully-fledged river suddenly emerges from the limestone. Having turned left, follow the main path carefully. At point 1138m it becomes very steep and climbs in zig-zags as far as the Tiergarten Hut at 1457m - a tough thousand feet! Not far above the Tiergarten Hut the path comes to an almost level section, the Herrengasse, then leaves this and once more climbs steeply, up the Wiesberg to the Wiesberg Haus. As you emerge into the high basin, you are rewarded by the sight of the great cirque of Dachstein peaks and ridges. A warm welcome at the Wiesberg Haus (1884m). Recover your rucksack, if you were lucky enough to be able to send it up.

The route is now more open and high-alpine in character. Soon you will see the Simony Hut in front of you, with its mountain chapel near it, both perched on great rock barrier, with the Hoher Ochsenkogel, like some monstrous beehive or dovecote to its right. The Simony Hut stands at 2203m, so you still have over 300m of ascent from the Wiesberg Haus, most of it towards the end. As you climb the final stages you will see at 2150m the Wildkar Hut, usually called the 'Simony Hotel', at the mouth of a cave: the first shelter to be built on the mountain, by Friedrich Simony in 1843.

At the Simony Hut a new world springs into view. The rock barrier on which it stands drops steeply to the south to meet the great Halstätter Gletscher (glacier) that sweeps down from the base of the Hoher Dachstein's rock tower. The hut was built in 1878-9 and enlarged several times, the latest being in 1964, by which time it was

71

looking rather shabby. (6hrs from Lahn.)

(The ascent of the Hoher Dachstein involves a crevassed glacier-crossing of 2¹/₄hrs to reach the Seethaler Hut (formerly the Dachsteinwarte Hut, at 2740m Cat. I, sleeps 8, but only in emergency). From here 'moderately difficult' climbing, with fixed ropes and iron spikes. 250m of ascent. 1hr. Roping-up advised.)

To continue the walk, return nearly 1km the way you came. A path to the Gjaid Alm goes off to the right, a pleasant, rambling path below the Tauben-Kogel. Only 3 or 4km. So why not leave your bag at the Gjaid Alm and climb the Taubenkogel?

Back 10-15mins the way you've come, then left (south), keeping 'Oberfeld' on your left. Gradually bear right (west) to point 1998m. Then south again until you are immediately below a saddle above the steep eastern flank of the Taubenkogel. Up to this (with care), then go north and a little east to the summit (2301m): triangulation point, Austrian style - a sort of wooden tripod. An extraordinarily rewarding viewpoint - the Krippenstein (NE), the Halstätter See, the Simony Hut area, and the Hoher Dachstein itself. Return same route: the Taubenkogel is precipitous on every other side.

Your next goal is the Schönberg Alm (1346m) with the entrance to the Dachstein Ice-Caves. On your route lies the Krippenstein Berghotel (2047m with 100 beds). You can keep your distance from this monstrosity by following a less obvious path keeping well to its right (red waymarks). It is extremely pleasant country to walk over.

The Dachstein Ice-Caves, very fully developed and with all kinds of Gordon-Craig lighting-effects, are an astonishing experience not to be missed.

Finally, a picturesque path north-west down to the valley and the village of Obertraun, at the SE end of the Halstätter See, about 4km by road from your starting point at Lahn.

(1964. Lahn-Wiesberg Haus, also 1978.)

A Personal Note: I have great affection for this walk as it was my first in the Austrian mountains, and especially for the Tauben-kogel, my first Austrian summit, and indeed only my second outside Britain, the first having been Gausta, in Norway, twenty-six years earlier, in 1938. (You might call me a late-developer.) It was a solitary walk, as I had been attending a conference near Salzberg. I

Gosaukamm Pinnacles

returned home to tell my wife she would love it, and ever since then we have visited Austria in summer together, either with friends or on our own. We visited the Dachstein group together in 1978 and 1979.

2. ROUND THE GOSAUKAMM (3 days walking)
(Gablonzer Hut (1532m Cat. II) - Grosser Donnerkogel (2054m) - Austriaweg - Theodor-Körner Hut (1454m Cat. I) Austriaweg - Hofpürgl Hut (1705m Cat. I) - Steigl Pass (2015m) - Steigl Way - Gosausee Dam.)

The *Gosaukamm ('Comb' - like the 'Crib' in 'Crib Goch') or Salzburg Dolomites, forming the extreme north-west arm of the Dachstein massif, is a jagged range of Dolomite-like peaks about 6km long and with some six or seven major tops of over 2000m, and innumerable other towers and pinnacles. High-level paths enable the walker to circumnavigate it at about 1400m with a 2000m pass. Several summits can be reached with scrambling.*

Start from the dam at the north-west end of the lake (large, long-stay car park) by taking the Gosaukammbahn (cable-car) to within 300m walking of the Gablonzer Hut (1522m Cat. II). In clear weather the walk to the Zwieselalm Höhe (1585m), a celebrated viewpoint to the north, is rewarding as an extra. *(We* could see no further than the nearest cow!)

For the round walk, leave the hut on the good path south-west (with impressive profiles of the north-east cliffs to your left) up to the Obere Törlecksattel (1594m) and beyond this to the Untere Törlecksattel (1575m). The route to the top of the Grosser Donnerkogel (2054m) forks left here and traverses slightly east of south, rising to 1866m, at the foot of a rock spur. Round this to the left and up much more steeply, but never harder than the easy way down off an English limestone crag, to the intensely dramatic summit at 2054m. The lake, over 1100m below, seems to lie at your feet. Romantic views of the Gosaukamm's *Gipfelmeer* (Sea of Peaks) as the German guidebook poetically expresses it, stretch to the Bischofsmütze (2459m) 4km away.

Return to the fork at the Untere Törlecksattel. On your way down you can see your next hut, the Theodor-Körner Hut, beyond and below you, due south

(There is a harder route, partly 'protected', that forks due south from the Gr.

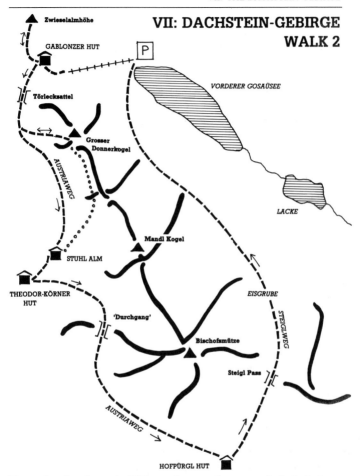

VII: DACHSTEIN-GEBIRGE
WALK 2

▲ Zwieselalmhöhe

GABLONZER HUT

P

VORDERER GOSAÜSEE

Törlecksattel

Grosser
Donnerkogel

AUSTRIAWEG

LACKE

Mandl Kogel

STUHL ALM

THEODOR-KÖRNER
HUT

EISGRUBE

STEIGLWEG

'Durchgang'

Bischofsmütze

Steigl Pass

AUSTRIAWEG

HOFPÜRGL HUT

Donnerkogel path at point 2025m, and goes to the next peak, the Steinriesen Kogel (2043m) and thence via the Kleine Weitscharte to the Theodor-Körner Hut.)

The Austria Way contours almost level between 1400m and 1500m to the Stuhl Alm (1461m) - a beautiful route, and easy, except for sticky limestone mud, like the so-called 'Derbyshire Cream', after rain. Just beyond the alm is the idyllic Theodor-Körner Hut (1454m Cat. I) nestling among the trees of the Schattenleitenkopf (1466m). It is small, cosy and homely: earth-closet in the woods, rain-water butt for washing, open-air wood-burning stove for the laundry. (If it is full there is accommodation at the Stuhl Alm.)

Next morning continue on the Austria Way walking gently up with the Bischofsmütze straight before you, past a hunting-lodge, then bearing right and going steeply up a gully called the *Durchgang* ('through-way') to a little, but important pass. Here we say good-bye to the SW face of the Gosaukamm and wide views open up to the south. The Austria Way continues due south, contouring to point 1633m, then swings, still contouring, though climbing slowly, in a huge S-bend below the Bischofsmütze to the Hofpürgl Hut (1705m Cat. I), which is visible ahead for a long time with the Hoher Dachstein as background. The hut is large, well-known, and easily accessible from the south. Since our visit it has been further enlarged and has become 'a self-service hotel/restaurant'. It is an Alpine Training Centre and attracts many day visitors. South from the hut the Rossbrand (see Radstädter Tauern, Walk 5. Additional walk from Radstadt) hides the Enns valley, and beyond it can be seen the tops of the Radstädter Tauern.

(This hut is the base for climbing the Bischofsmütze (2459m). This very popular ascent is beyond the scope of this book. Its 'moderately difficult' easiest route is harder than the easiest route up the Hoher Dachstein, and is unprotected.)

Next day take a good path almost due north to the Steigl Pass (2015m), at first stonily up a big corrie, later a rock ledge, with fixed rope. From the pass you can still see the hut. To the west is the Bischofsmütze, to the east the exciting-looking ridge leading to the Steiglkogel (2205m).

(This summit is $^3/4$hr from the pass, an exposed route with fixed ropes.)

North of the Steigl Pass the Steigl Way goes gently down, at first through a rocky valley - limestone walking at its best. Ahead is the sharp Gabelkogel (1909m). As we approach this we enter the Eisgrube, a deep hollow and one of the most romantically rugged parts of the whole walk. Emerging on to a more open section we can actually see all the way to our starting point, the Gablonzer Hut. There is now 3km of almost level path between the high peaks on the left and the lower tier of cliffs falling towards the lake on the right.

On the site of a former alm is a curious little chapel built to the memory of all who have lost their lives on the Gosaukamm, but especially to a young woman who was killed in abseiling off the Däumling (a rock pinnacle), which she had just been the first woman to climb

Finally, steeply and somewhat knee-wreckingly down to the dam. We have earned the right to appreciate the classic view from this, admired by every tourist. At the same time indulge in gazing up at the Grosser Donnerkogel, which from here appears to be absolutely inaccessible. You have just completed 'one of the hundred best walks in the Alps', and climbed one of the Salzburg Dolomites into the bargain. (1979)

VIII: The Totes Gebirge
(AVE Group 15)

The Name: The Dead Mountains! The name probably arises from the barrenness of most of the high plateau. It is not known for certain when the name was first used or came into general use.

Boundaries of the Group: The Offenseebach - the Griesseneckbach - Moosau - Habernau - Hetzau - Ödseen - Bernerau - the Weissenach to its junction with the Steyr - the Steyr to its junction with the Teichl - the Teichl - Pyhrnn Pass - the Enns from Liezen to Trautenfels - Klacheu - Bad Mitterndorf - Pötschenhöhe - Bad Goisern - the Traun to its junction with the Offenseebach.

The Totes Gebirge group lies north-east of the Dachstein Group.

Its main feature is the huge limestone plateau that gives the group its name. Imagine the Ingleborough plateau magnified to twelve times its area, lifted to a height of some 1400m-2000m and tilted from north-east to south-west, and you will have some idea of this challenging high level wilderness. Its encircling precipices offer immense scope to the rock-climber, while the plateau is a wild and testing place for the walker.

The walks described are on the central area of the plateau and include both northern and southern approaches. They could be linked to make one expedition.

WARNING: The plateau has innumerable sink-holes ('Dolinen' as they are called locally) which offer as serious a danger to walkers as do crevasses in glaciers. While they do not occur actually *on* the waymarked paths they do occur very near them, and, of course, if you leave the waymarked path you can fall into them without any warning at all.

1. A NORTH-SOUTH CROSSING OF THE TOTES GEBIRGE

(3 days) (Almtalerhaus (714m Cat. II) - Welser Hut (1815m Cat. I) - Pühringer Hut (1638m Cat. I) - Grundlsee.)

There are trains to Grünau-im-Almtal and buses as far as Jägersimmerl (Habernau) up the Längau valley (due south). Here

VIII. TOTES GEBIRGE

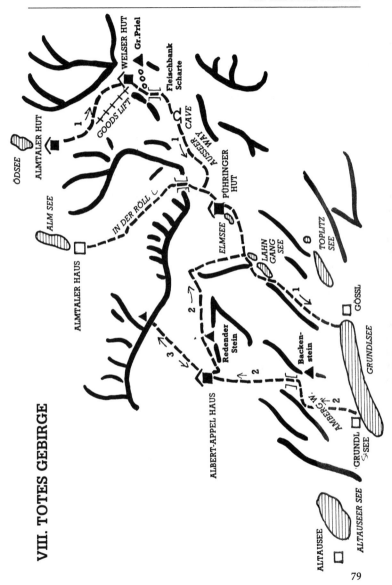

sharp turn left (east) and about 5 km to the Almtaler Hut. If motorised you can drive all the way to this comfortable valley hut of the Wels Section of the AV. (Unless a new campsite has been set up, camping in this area presents problems. Most of the land is privately owned by chamois hunters.)

From the hut south, climbing gently up the Hinterer Hetzautal to the bottom station of the Welser Hut's goods cable-way. If you can possibly cope with the telephone in German, do send your rucksack up on this: you may be asked to unload the empty beer-crates and load on the full ones, too! From here the path climbs steeply to the hut, wooded at first, then rocky and bare. You may see many chamois and will certainly see black salamanders on the rocks. More seriously, there are black adders in the Totes Gebirge! A final big zig-zag brings you to the hut. If it seems rather coldly comfortless in poor weather, remember that it is the fourth of its name. The first was a mere forester's hut, demolished about the time that the Wels Section obtained the lease of the Almtalerhaus. The second, the result of the enthusiasm of Sepp Huber, was destroyed by an avalanche in 1923 after barely three years' existence. The third was damp and without adequate foundations: eventually the floor sloped so steeply that the plates slipped off the tables. The present hut, built in record time in 1968, is modern in materials, design and structure. The situation is magnificent.

Leave the hut on its south side. Almost immediately you encounter a ladder. Then up a stony corrie to the Fleischbanke, with a steep section of rock, the Hausbauernband, furnished with a series of iron ladders and fixed ropes, leading to the Fleischbanksattel at 2122m.

(To the left (east) the summit of the Grosser Priel, 2515m, the highest point in the Totes Gebirge, is about 1¹/₂km away and 400m higher.)

The route to the Pühringer Hut leads right (west). (Note that *P.H.* on a rock here means 'Pühringer Hut' NOT 'Prielschutzhaus'.) Now begins the 5km walk south-west over the totally barren limestone plateau. Keep strictly to the waymarked path, as the plateau abounds in deadly sink-holes. (Dolinen). After about 1km you pass a cave (Höhle) that can be a life-saver in bad weather. Indeed this whole walk, though presenting no problems on a clear, sunny day, can become a very serious proposition in a blizzard, even in August - and this is written from experience! Whatever the guidebooks say, the waymark beyond the cave tells you it is another 3hrs to the Pühringer Hut. (Many of the waymarks are necessarily on the ground and are soon hidden by snow.)

The path, known as the Ausseerweg, has many bends and many ups and downs. Eventually a vast rising 'ditch' the *Aufg'hackert*, leads up to the Rotkogelsattel - the final pass. From here down steeply to join the path from the Röllsattel, then less than 1km, easily to the Pühringer Hut (1638m Cat. I) by the Elmsee, another hut of the Wels Section, comfortable and welcoming.

An alternative way to this hut from the north is to keep straight on south up the Alm Valley at Jägersimmerl/Habernau to the Seehaus on the Almsee (parking). From here a good path, walled on both sides by magnificent limestone cliffs, leads 'In der Röll' to the bottom of the Sepp Huber Steig (left).

(This well-marked and in places protected path leads up to the Röllsattel.)

From the Röllsattel, good walking through hummocky limestone country brings you to the junction with the Ausseer Way and so to the hut. (This could be used to make a round walk, especially if you have left a car at the Almtalerhaus.)

To go down on the south side of the massif, walk south-west past the Elmsee (1620m) to the Elmgrube (hunting-lodge) and continue in the same direction past the little Hinterer Lahngang See (1495m) and the much larger and very beautiful Vorderer Lahngang See (1489m). After the lakes down more steeply, though a rocky 'gate', the Drausengatterl, and so eventually down to the Grundlsee at just over 700m.

(If you have a car at the Almtalerhaus it is not sensible to come down on this side of the mountains unless forced to do so by bad weather. The return journey by public transport is complex: 1) Get to Bad Aussee; 2) Train from Bad Aussee to Gmunden Station (70km picturesque ride); 3) special trams from Gmunden Station to the town; 4) Bus to Grünau, or to Jägersimmerl if you are very lucky; otherwise finish by taxi or a *very* long walk.)   (1972)

2. GRUNDLSEE - ALBERT-APPEL-HAUS (1660m Austrian Tourist Association) - PÜHRINGER HUT (1638m Cat. I) GRUNDLSEE

There is a campsite at Gössl at the east end of the Grundlsee. Start walking at the village of Grundlsee on the north shore, near the western end. You can park near Wirtshaus Schrainl. The path, the Almberg Way, climbs through forest almost due north, then more interestingly up the west side of a forested cwm with fine views to the east of the steep south spur of the Backenstein. Then bear right, past a cave under the Almbergkar, then left (north) again to emerge soon on the plateau, which here has quite a different character from the eastern plateau. It consists of alm pastures and broken woodland.

The path continues almost due north to the Brunnwiesen Alm (1579m) and beyond it past the little Naturfreunde Hut, the Heueralm (1660m), to the now visible Albert-Appel-Haus (1660m), rather 'grand', but pleasant. (Probably no reduction for AV membership.)

After some bends at the start the path from here to the Pühringer Hut runs west-east just north of the Redender Stein (1902m: 'Speaking Stone' - test its echo for yourself) and further over extremely pleasant limestone country to a little tarn, the Wieslacke (1829m). After this it has to go round the northern end of the Wildgössl (2066m) and then south-east and south under the splendid crags of the Salzofen (2072m) to the Elmgrube (hunting-lodge). Here turn sharply north-east, and the path leads directly over a slight eminence called Emils Tränenhügel (Emil's Hill of Tears) to the Elmsee and the Pühringer Hut.

For the direct return to the Grundlsee, see Walk 1.   (1972)

3.   THE GROSSER WOISING (2064m)

Easily accessible from the Albert-Appel-Haus, this mountain, seen from the north, is a mighty rock colossus. Its name is probably from a Slav word, wysok, *meaning 'high'.*

The mountain lies north-east of the Albert-Appel-Haus, with a marked path all the way over increasingly rough ground, very bare and rocky in the end. No problems. Good views.

As this summit is only 2¹/₂hrs from the hut, you can easily make a round trip to visit the Redender Stein (1902m see Walk 2), easily accessible from the south-west and worthwhile because it is such a good central viewpoint.

It can, of course, also be visited by making a detour from the path to the Pühringer Hut (Walk 2).   (1972)

IX: The Ennstaler Alps (Gesäuse)
(AVE Group 16)

The Name: The mountain group simply takes its name from the valley of the River Enns which flows through it. The "Gesäuse", which often appears as a supplementary title for the group is actually the name of a wooded gorge 10 miles/16km long through which the River Enns drops 505ft/154m, surging between the rugged limestone crags, and the word 'Gesäuse' is onomatopoeically derived from the sound of the rushing waters.

The Boundaries of the Group: Windischgarsten - Dambach - Hengstpaß - Laussa - Enns to Hieflau - Erzbach - Präblichl - Vordernberger Bach - Mur from Leoban to St. Michael - Liesing/Paltental to its junction with the Enns - Liezen - Pyhrnpaß - Winischgarsten.

The area, which is the most easterly in this guidebook, contains much of interest, including the unique Erzberg, a mountain cut into vast terraces by opencast mining. It is the largest deposit of spathic iron ore (siderite) in Europe and has been mined since ancient times. The picturesque town of Eisernerz below the mountain has a remarkable fortified church.

The walks described here are based on Admont, famous for its Benedictine abbey (founded 1074) and especially for the abbey library, which survived a disastrous fire in 1865. At one time a popular resort for the Viennese, Admont now wears a faintly dilapidated air, not lacking in a certain charm. There is an unpretentious campsite at Hall, a suburb north of the river. Some 3km north of the town there rises, like a mighty defensive fortification, the Haller Mauern, the Walls of Hall, a mountain range to which two of our three walks lead us. The third walk is on the mountains that rise immediately north of the Gesäuse Gorge itself.

1. THE ROHRAUERHAUS (1308m) and the GROSSER PYHRGAS (2244m)

Route: Admont - Zirnitz -Mühlau (car park) Gstattmaier (Niedere

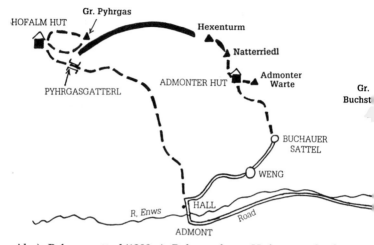

Alm) - Pyhrgasgatterl (1308m) - Rohrauerhaus - Hofersteig - Großer
Pyhrgas. *Descent:* Hofalmsattel - Rohrauerhaus. Then as ascent.

Take the road north from Admont - or from Hall, if you are camping
there - via Zirnitz to Mühlau. If motorised you may drive this far,
parking at the end of the public road just beyond the tiny Mühlau
Electricity Works and by a wayside shrine. Take a rough road
running level through fields WNW, past the entrance to the very
'private' Sattleralm to the foot of the much steeper open pastures of
the Gstattmaier, whose cattle-buildings lie at 913m. You now enter
woods on a real mountain path and can soon refresh yourself at a
spring whose drinking water flows through a wooden trough.
Beyond this, notice, but do not follow, a path going off R to the
Scheiblingstein (2197m). Above this the path may be tricky to
follow: watch the waymarks! You meet a forestry road and eventually
come up on a broad ridge where there is a great bare patch and a
forestry road. Do not be tempted to follow this but find the
continuation of the path. In 1991 the footpath sign had been damaged
by fire and the word "Rohrauerhaus" was virtually illegible.
Following this you lose a little height, then gain it once more to a
watershed that forms the state boundary between Steiermark (Styria)
and Oberösterreich (Upper Austria). The boundary is marked by a

IX: ENNSTALER ALPS

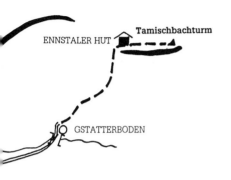

fence and a little gate, the Pyhrgasgatterl named on the map. In a few minutes you reach the Rohrauerhaus (1308m). This is a hut of the Naturfreunde (TVN) more obviously approached from Spital, from which it is the goal of many day visitors. At night it is remote and quiet. (3hrs from Mühlau.)

The Großer Pyhrgas (2244m) your goal in the morning, is the highest and most westerly summit of the Haller Mauern, which runs as a rocky crescent from this top via the Scheiblingstein (2167m), the Kreuzmauer (2091m), several lesser tops and the impressive Bärenkarmauer or Hexenturm (2172m) to the Natterriedl (2065m) at its eastern end, above the Admonter Hut.

The route given here is described in the German guidebook *Nur für Geübte* (only for the experienced), but it presents no very serious difficulties in good weather. It begins NE through woods, then NNW with the name "Hofersteig", climbing steep open slopes with stony terraces. Away to the right are the horrendous SE cliffs. The path is steep in places and, as a reminder of potential danger, there is a memorial plaque on a rock which records the death there of a member of the Naturfreunde, a retired headmistress, Frau Emilie Kipperling, on 22 September 1927. The path climbs diagonally up stonier slopes, quite scrambly in parts and with three fixed chains, to join the ridge that comes up from the WSW. From here it is a mere 20mins to the summit. (About 3hrs from the hut.)

The views from the summit, which is marked by a large metal cross, are justly celebrated. Along the range to the east are the other tops of the Haller Mauern, rocky and steep; to the NW, Spital lies some 1600m below.

For descent it is easier to keep to the WSW ridge, though this would be tedious in ascent. Partway down a sign points towards a cave, 20mins away. At the Hofalmsattel (saddle) go left. (Right goes to the Hofalm Hut and ultimately to Spital.) From here an almost level path leads straight back to the Rohrauerhaus. To descend to Admont reverse the ascent. (1991)

2. THE ADMONTER HAUS (1723m), THE ADMONTER WARTE (1804m) and THE NATTERRIEDL (2065m).

Route: Buchauer Sattel (861m) (Park by Schwarzbauer, a disused farmstead) - Grabneralm (1395m) - Admonter Haus (1723m) - Admonter Warte (1804m)/Natterriedl (2065m).

Admonter Haus: The walk begins at the Buchauer Sattel (861m) on the St. Gallen road NE of Weng.

This can be reached by car or bus from Admont. Park near the Schwarzbauer, a disused farmstead, and start walking on Route 636. Cross a field to join a rough forestry road at 900m, which zig-zags up to 1200m, the waymarked path once cutting a corner. (Watch the waymarks carefully!) After a hairpin bend at 1200m the slightly rising track traverses a section which would be threatened by avalanches in snowy weather. Cross a small stream and a larger one. A bend left, then soon after, one to the right and you climb to the Grabneralm (1395m), an attractive, oldish building where refreshments are obtainable. Above the alm the route is steep and can be muddy, becoming stonier after a time and you are soon rewarded with your first sight of the Admonter Haus high above you on its saddle, the Grabnertörl (1723m): a good and hospitable hut.

The Admonter Warte (1804m): Opposite the door of the hut rises the Admonter Warte, only about 80m higher than the hut. It is steep but perfectly easy, climbed on loose, grotty limestone with some fixed rope protection. The view is notably rewarding.

The Natterriedl (2065m) (Literally 'The Little Adder-Marsh': I saw neither adders nor marsh!) From the hut this, the most easterly summit of the Haller Mauern, presents no difficulties. A short walk leads to an easy 'pitch' of about 20ft with a more or less unnecessary fixed rope. Then the path runs almost level and fairly exposed behind the cliff visible from the hut, after which another 'pitch' with fixed rope leads to a little col. An easy zig-zag path now leads up open grassy slopes. Near its top, one branch of the path continues to traverse up left below a crag. This is the direct way to the Hexenturm (see below). An arrow directs you to the right. This takes you to the Mittagskogel (2042m) with a summit cross. For the Natterriedl (2065m) regain the path and continue to the summit: no cross, just a 'summit book' in a metal box on a spike.

(To go on to the Hexenturm, a more serious proposition, you have to lose 200m in height before climbing up to the summit at 2172m. A good head is needed; there are some fixed ropes and the route is slabby in places. Return the same way.)

For descent from the Natterriedl and then from the hut, reverse the ascent.(1991)

3. THE ENNSTALER HUT (1544m) and the TAMISCH-BACHTURM (2035m).

Route: Gstatterboden (577m) - Near the Gstatterbodenbauer - Niederscheibenalm - Butterbründl - Jagdhütte - Ennstaler Hut (1544m) - Tamischbachturm (2035m)

Start on the Admont-Hieflau road at the Gstatterboden, a small, picturesque spot chiefly consisting of forestry buildings - including a sawmill - a railway station, a hotel, and a chapel dedicated to St. Hubert. You can park here. The path goes past the chapel, through young forestry, crosses a forestry road, drops down to a stream, crosses this on a footbridge and climbs again to another forestry road. (In 1991 the footbridge had been swept away in the severe floods of that summer and it was necessary to go down the first forestry road, cross the stream on the main road bridge and then go up the second forestry road.) This stony, shelterless road climbs steadily but not steeply past the Gstatterbodenbauer to the Niederscheibenalm, gaining only about 300m in 2km of harsh walking. Here the route leaves the road. Notice a sign before you reach this alm: the forestry road goes right to Hieflau via the Hochscheibenalpe while the path (646) crosses alm pastures and then enters woods: if the weather is hot you will welcome a rest here,

Großer Buchstein

bearing in mind that though you have come about half the distance to the hut, you still have over 600m to climb. Presently you reach another rough and stony road. Go right on this until the path goes up *steeply* to the left just before the bottom station of the goods cableway to the hut. I don't know whether rucksacks can be sent up on this. It is easy to miss the way about here. At 1151m you cross yet another forestry road and the path gets steeper and steeper. At one point there is a magnificently photogenic view west of the Großer Buchstein (2224m). (At about this point walkers we met gave varying estimates of 'a good hour' and 'an hour and a half' to the hut.)

The next feature is a welcome spring, the Butterbründl, at about 1300m, soon followed by a sign giving 'one hour' to the hut. You will make some height on a fine and enjoyable section of the path that finds a way up through steep crags. The next sign says 'half-an-hour', and that is about right for the young and fit: it took us 45mins. This friendly and welcoming hut, situated on a picturesque saddle between the Tieflimauer and the Tamischbachturm commands wonderful views in every direction: the Buchstein group, the Enns valley, Hochtor, Lugauer and St. Gallen. Sunset behind the Buchstein is a sight to remember!

Compared with the strenuous climb to the hut the ascent of the Tamischbachturm, about 500m higher, is heartwarmingly easy - at first through woods and scrub, then out on open slopes and finally a slightly scrambly ridge with a superb surprise view of the precipitous and rugged north side. The all-round panoramic view from the summit is breathtaking and on a fine morning is incredibly beautiful, demanding a huge expenditure of colour film. Return to the hut and from the hut to Gstatterboden presents no problems except that of convincing those you meet of how far they have yet to go to reach the hut.   (1991)

X: The Rätikon Group
(AVE Group 25)

The Name: Although the name Rätikon in its Latin form *Retico Mons* is at least 1900 years old, it is only in the last hundred years or so that it has been applied and limited to the group of mountains which now bears it.

Boundaries of the Group: The Rätikon Group is in the shape of a rhombus whose corners are Feldkirch, St. Gallenkirch, Klosters and Landquart, and whose boundaries are in the north (Feldkirch-St. Gallenkirch) the Ill valley; in the east the Gargellan, Valzifenz and Schlappin valleys between St. Gallenkirch and Klosters; in the south the Landquart valley from Klosters to that river's junction with the Rhine at Landquart; and in the west the Rhine from its junction with the Landquart to its junction with the Ill.

The main ridge of the group forms the frontier between Austria and Liechtenstein in the west and Switzerland in the south. Thirty-three of the Rätikon's summits are over 2500m, and 36 between 2000m and 2500m, the highest, the Schesaplana (2965m) barely failing to reach the 3000m mark. The group's boundaries are purely orographic and geographic and within them is presented a wide variety of geological and geomorphological features. It therefore offers the mountain walker considerable scope, from easy walking to hard scrambling, plus the ascent of a snow peak, the Schesaplana, without the hazards of glaciation.

British walkers will probably find Bludenz or Schruns the most convenient bases, whether they come by road or rail. The walks described here assume Bludenz as base, a town steeped in mountaineering history, where in 1873 the German and Austrian Alpine Clubs (DAV and OeAV) united to form the German and Austrian Alpine Club (DOeAV). Two campsites are available, that in the suburb of Nüziders being particularly good.

1. ROUND THE LÜNERSEE

Drive, or catch the first bus, from Bludenz up the Brandnertal to the bottom station of the Lünerseebahn (1565m) whence the cable-car

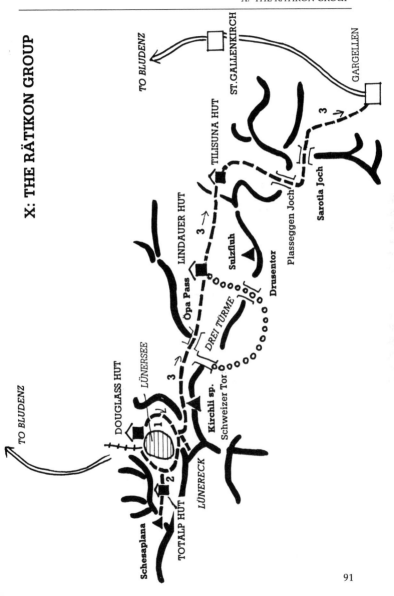

91

will take you up on to the Lünersee Dam (1979m). (Of course there is a path up these 400m if you are a purist.) The Lünersee is a natural lake whose capacity has been increased from 40 to 76 million cubic metres by the building of the dam. A few yards east of the top station of the cable-car (which actually lies on the natural rock lip of the lake) is the Douglass Hut (Cat. III) a replacement provided by the hydro-electric company for an earlier hut flooded when the dam was built. (The original hut, built in 1872 on the initiative of John Sholto Douglass, a British industrialist and mountaineer, was the first Alpine hut to be erected by the German Alpine Club.) The new hut is much used by day-tourists, but is quite cosy when the last cable-car has gone down.

Walk past the hut, east, across the dam (impressive!) and ascend the path beyond, keeping right at a fork: the left-hand path is a somewhat hairy route to the Heinrich-Hüter Hut. Although there is only about 100m of ascent the views across the Lünersee and of the towering Seekopf (2698m) on its far side are quite disproportionately rewarding. Once more keep right and continue clockwise round the lake to the Lünersee Alm (milk usually on sale). As the plain round-the-lake walk takes only about 2hrs a worthwhile addition is to follow the path south from the alm, keeping right, for the Cavell-Joch (2238m) on the Swiss frontier. From this follow the ridge west to the Lünereck (2297m; national boundary stone) with splendid views of the Schesaplana to the WNW.and of the rocky frontier peaks of the Kirchlispitzen, Drusenfluh and Sulzfluh to the ESE. Return to the lake-side path and continue, almost level, around the shore to your starting point. (The last cable-car goes down at 5pm.)

(1974/83)

2. THE SCHESAPLANA (2965m)

(NOTE. The potential difficulties of this very popular mountain, the highest in the group, are not to be underestimated. It is a snow mountain, and though there is no glacier on the southern approach there is permanent snow, so suitable equipment is necessary. Difficulties are increased if snow cover is deep or in mist. It is no place for inexperienced or badly equipped tourists.)

Go west from the Douglass Hut and follow the lakeside path for about 1100m where the Schesaplana ascent branches half-right. The

The Three Towers from the Lindauer Hut

route, waymarked red/yellow is partly a made path and partly a trodden-out track. It lies below the south flank of the Seekopf, climbing west up the steep little valley of the stream coming down from the Zirmenseeli or Totalpseeli, (Seeli = little lake, i.e. tarn) and eventually entering the high, rather flat corrie of that little lake which may well be invisible under ice and snow. (2318m, and 1¹/₂hrs from the hut more or less.) Here you may fork left (south) to the Totalp Hut or continue more to the right, leaving the hut to be visited on the way down. Even at this height snow-cover, or at least patchy snow, is likely. Continue to the highest levels of the Tote Alp (2650m) - whose name, 'Dead Alm' gives a true notion of its barrenness - and then swing half-right (NW and N) climbing steeply to the high horseshoe-shaped corrie that lies SE of the summit ridge. This is usually snow-filled even in mid and late summer. The snow basin is traversed high up from right to left on a steep slope. The final ridge then gives easy walking to the summit with its extensive views.

(To continue to the Strassburger Hut on the north side involves crossing the Brandner Glacier, sometimes badly iced in late summer and not wholly free from crevasses. Only for those with glacier experience and equipment!)

The descent to the Douglass Hut reverses the ascent. The steep lip of the upper snow basin may be intimidating, snow steps may by now be soft and broken by careless walkers. The Totalp Hut (2385m Cat. I) a small, simple hut originally put up by the hydro-electric company for its workers, and wardened in the summer season, provides a welcome break and refreshment on the return journey, with fine views of the upper part of the ascent route and of the Lünersee below. The rest of the descent should present no problems. Note that the summit of the Schesaplana is almost exactly 1000m above the Lünersee, so time your walk accordingly.   (1974)

3.   DOUGLASS HUT TO GARGELLEN

Route: Douglass Hut (1979m Cat. III) - Verajoch (2330m) - Schweizer Tor (2137m) - Öfa Pass (2291m) - Lindauer Hut (1744m Cat. I) - Schwarze Scharte (2336m) - Tilisuna Hut (2208m Cat. I) - ascent of Sulzfluh (2818m) - Plasseggen Joch (2354m) - Sarotla Joch (2389m) - Gargellen (1424m) .

A classic, this, for a three-day walk.

Weißplatte from Sulzfluh path

Start from the Douglass Hut round the lake in either direction as far as the Lünersee Alm: the official route (waymarked red / white / red and avoiding gain and loss of height) is anti-clockwise. After the Alm leave the lake behind you and soon keep left past a little customs hut up to the Verajoch or Verajöchl (2330m). Admire the north face of the Kirchlispitzen (2551m) with its climbs of all grades from I to VI. View to the west of the Schesaplana and east to the Drusenfluh (2827m). Continue down to the customs hut at the Schweizer Tor, the 'Swiss Gate', an enormous rock portal between the Kirchlispitzen and the Drusenfluh, said to have been a favourite smugglers' route in the past.

(A longer and more energetic variation of the route here described is to go through the 'Gate' into Switzerland, take the path SE (*not* SW), traverse pastures and scree basins until a sharp turn north leads up to the Drusentor (2343m), a romantically rocky pass between the Drei Türme and the Sulzfluh, after having to lose and regain some 200m in height. From the Drusentor an interesting path leads down to the Lindauer Hut. Add about 2hrs to your time for this.)

From the Schweizer Tor up again to the Öfa Pass (2291m) whence the Lindauer Hut is visible, 3km away and 500m lower; down the Sporentobel (a heat-trap), past the prosperous looking Spora Alm to the hut - large, and friendly and boasting a justly celebrated Alpine Garden.

(Determined scramblers with a day to spare can climb from here two of the Three Towers (Drei Türme) that form the picturesque backdrop to the hut. Start on the Drusentor path and do not turn right until you reach the waymarked path. The ascent is strenuous, and the 'big' and 'middle' towers are for *experienced* scramblers. The 'little' tower is the preserve of rock-climbers .)

Make an early start from the Lindauer Hut in order to get up the Bilken Grat before the sun reaches it. This section of the walk is one of the most beautiful of the whole of the Rätikon High Level route. Start through the Porzalengawald, the woods on whose edge the hut stands. The route zig-zags scenically over limestone, then up a section of volcanic rock and finally, after much floral interest also, to the black serpentine of the Schwarze Scharte (Black Pass, 2336m) from whence - when you have sufficiently appreciated the outlook - the path drops about 100m to the Tilisuna Hut (2208m). Early arrival here makes a rucksack-free ascent of the Sulzfluh (2818m) an essential, easy, and one of the most magnificent of high alpine walks!

From the hut W and SW over high pastures and then easily and rewardingly over limestone pavements. The route is clear and presents no problems, and the summit offers a glorious view to the west of the whole main Rätikon ridge as far as the Schesaplana. The first recorded ascent was in 1782, when two local priests visited the summit and the mountain's caves.

(It is possible to ascend the Sulzfluh from the Lindauer Hut en route for the Tilisuna Hut but only the experienced should attempt this. It is strenuous and more difficult to follow, and the 'Rachen' - a long, high corrie, is usually snow-filled. It can easily take $4^1/2$hrs from the hut to summit, whereas the direct hut to hut route is only $2^1/2$-3hrs. Be warned!)

Next morning, leave the Tilisuna Hut, the second highest in the Rätikon, built 1879 and lying among spacious high-alpine pastures about 100m above the little Tilisuna Lake. Go SW over pastures up to, *but not over,* the Gruben Pass (2241m), and continue S on the eastern slopes of the Weissplatte and Scheienfluh to the Plasseggen Pass (2354m); cross this into Switzerland, where a fine traverse path leads to the Sarotla Pass (2389m) over which we return to Austria. The descent to Gargellen runs SE on the right of the Sarotla Tal. Watch the route carefully at the Obere Räbi Alm.

From Gargellen buses run to Schruns whence you can catch a train back to Blundenz.

(To shorten the last day, if short of time, descend north from the Tilisuna Hut directly to Tschagguns/Schruns.)　　　　(1974/83)

XI: The Silvretta Group
(AVE Group 26)

The Boundaries of the Group: St. Gallenkirch - R. Ill to Partenen - Zeinisjoch - Zeinisbach - Paznauntal to Ischgl - Fimbertal - Fimberpass - Val Chöglias - Val Sinestra - R. Inn from junction with Brancla Bach to junction with Susasca - Val Susasca - Flüelapass - Davos - Wolfgang - Laretbach - Klosters - Schlappinbach - Schlappiner Joch - Valzifenzbach - Gargellen Tal - St. Gallenkirch.

The Silvretta forms the middle section of a crescent whose 'horns' are the Rätikon and Samnaun Groups and within which - like 'the old moon in the new moon's arms' - lies the Ferwall Group. Its main ridge, continuing that of the Rätikon, forms the Austro-Swiss frontier. Unlike the Rätikon and Ferwall Groups it is quite heavily glaciated on its northern side, and even has several glaciers on its southern, Swiss, side. The group is therefore among the most spectacular of Austro-Swiss mountains, while its high-level routes take on a serious character.

Access from the north by road is provided by the miraculously engineered Silvretta Hochalpenstrasse (High Alpine Road) - toll from Partenen in the west to Galtur in the east, and thousands of tourists gain a 'Silvretta Experience' simply by driving this road. Drive - or take the bus - to Bielerhöhe (2034m), the highest point of the road, at the northern end of the Silvretta Stausee. Avoid parking on the vast car park provided for day-visitors. There is parking at the start of the path to the Wiesbadener Hut for those going that way.

1. THE WIESBADENER HUT (2443m Cat. I) AND PIZ BUIN (3312m)

From Bielerhöhe the path to the hut follows the east side of the lake to its end and then climbs steadily up the Ochsental SE and SSE to the hut, with splendid views the whole way of the three thousanders ahead. (An alternative leaves the lake about half way along and traverses the west slopes of the Hohes Rad at a rather higher level

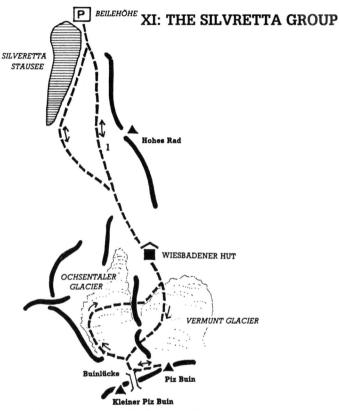

XI: THE SILVRETTA GROUP

to rejoin the main path a little way below the hut.)

The situation of the Wiesbadener Hut is scenically quite outstanding. It is virtually surrounded by peaks, while to the south and south-west the Vermunt and Ochsentaler Glaciers add beauty and drama, the latter falling steeply between the hut and the Silvretta Horn (3244m) the former leading more gently towards Piz Buin. None of the peaks accessible from this hut is ungraded walking; three however are only Grade I and are therefore available to any well experienced alpine mountain walker. These are: Vermuntkopf (2851m 1$^{1/2}$hrs); Ochsenkopf (east peak 3057m - the easiest three thousander from this hut; but involving permanent snow on the little Tiroler Glacier; 2¹/₂hrs); and Hohes Rad (2934m - one of the finest easy mountains with a great view in the eastern alps. 3-3¹/₂hrs).

The ascent of Piz Buin is not at all difficult (Grade I-II) in good conditions, but it does involve some easy rock climbing and some glacier-crossing. It should therefore not be attempted solo by walkers and a rope should be carried. The German guidebook also regards crampons and ice-axe as imperative.

Start from the hut due south over moraine fields to the edge of the Vermunt Glacier. This is gently sloping, but although easy, it has some crevasses in it, so it is safer to rope up here rather than wait for the rock. (Not everyone does so, however!) Ascend the glacier south in the direction of the Vermunt Pass to a height of about 2700m, then turn right, SW, and climb more steeply - beware of crevasses here - to the Wiesbadner Grätle. This rock band must be climbed (Grade I or II according to conditions and the route taken). The easiest way up consists chiefly of a traverse rising from right to left with plenty of rock spikes. You can move together here, simply clipping into slings dropped over spikes for protection. The rock section leads to the upper basin of the Ochsentaler Glacier. SW up this - again with danger of crevasses! - to the Buinlücke (3056m) the snow-pass between the Grosser and Kleiner Piz Buin. Seen from this side the Kleiner Piz Buin (3255m) is a narrow, shapely pyramid. Its easiest ascent is Grade II rock-climbing, so is outside the scope of this book. The Grosser Piz Buin, on our left as we approach the Buinlücke, is easier, though higher (3312m). From the Buinlücke turn left and go diagonally (NE) up scree, snow-patches and tracks until a steep rock groove is reached, called the Kamin or Chimney. Although in good conditions this can be easier than the Grätle, it can be nasty, especially if iced, and if the rope has now been taken off, re-roping is strongly recommended. From the top of the Kamin the walk up the 'roof' to the summit is easy.

The view is rewarding: SW, across the Buinlücke, Kleiner Piz Buin rises gracefully against the backdrop of La Cudèra Glacier and the Verstankla Horn (3298m) in Switzerland; E and ENE the main Silvretta ridge with its snow-flecked rock peaks and extensive glaciers stretches away from us; N, the north ridge of Piz Buin leads the eye down to the Ochsental with the Wiesbadener Hut at its head and the Silvretta Stausee at its foot, while to its right the cliffs of the Hohes Rad (2943m) rise darkly but elegantly.

Descend to the Buinlücke by the ascent route - with special care at the Kamin. Then, to avoid having to reverse the rock-pitches on the Grätle and to gain some impressive glacier scenery, you may, if you have sufficient glacier experience, descend the Ochsentaler Glacier. From the Buinlücke traverse SW under the N side of the Kleiner Piz Buin in order to reach the left side of the glacier. It is *essential* to keep to the left in order to avoid the ice-fall, and though there are usually the tracks of other parties to be followed, even here there are often many crevasses. Below the ice-fall go diagonally right at about 2600m, descending E and NE to the moraine-saddle at about 2570m south of the 'Grüne Kuppe' (2579m). From here a little track leads diagonally right (SE) down on to the tongue of the Vermunt Glacier. Cross this (E) to the other side, then go left (N) on tracks to the hut. (1974)

The crossings to other huts from the Wiesbadener Hut are for the most part glaciated and must be attempted only by parties with good glacier experience. Most users of this book will therefore go down to Bielerhöhe by the normal hut path.

XII: The Ferwall Group
(AVE Group 28)

The Name: This is sometimes spelt *Verwall* (e.g. on the Kompass Wanderkarte) but the older form *Ferwall is* preferable.
Boundaries of the Group: Bludenz - Klostertal - Stuben - Arlberg Pass - Stanzer Tal as far as Wiesberg - Paznauntal - Zeinis Bach - Zeinisjoch - Partenen - the River Ill to Bludenz.

The Ferwall Group lies primarily between the steep and often forbidding Lechtal Group to its north and the higher, glaciated Silvretta to its south, though it may be regarded as a continuation of the latter's western and central parts. In shape it is a triangle whose base is formed by the Klostertal and Stanzertal, and whose apex is the Zeinisjoch by the Kops reservoir in the south. The centre of the group, the Winterjöchl, is of European significance, as it forms a watershed between feeders of the Rhine and those of the Danube. Geologically the area is formed primarily of gneiss and hornblende, the former having a lighter colour and forming softer shapes, the latter darker and sharper.

Free of the steep, insecure rock of the Lechtal Alps and the glaciers of the Silvretta, the Ferwall provides an ideal terrain for the mountain walker, with many worthy summits, including the Hoher Riffler, 3162m - the second highest summit in the group by a mere 8m. (The Kuchenspitze, the highest, is 3170m, and its easiest ascents are Grade II climbing.)

The most significant summits lie in the eastern half, as do five of the group's eight Alpenverein huts.

For the Briton approaching from the north St. Anton offers the best base for exploring the eastern Ferwall. There is no campsite at St. Anton, but so geared for winter downhill skiing is this over-expanded and mechanised little town that summer visitors are likely to find accommodation that welcomes them and does not overcharge. St. Anton is easy to reach by rail and also by road, since the building of the Arlberg road tunnel has eliminated the crawl over the Arlberg Pass. Two walks are described here, but these

XII: FERWALL GROUP

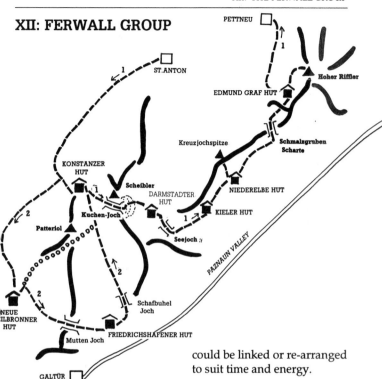

could be linked or re-arranged
to suit time and energy.

1. HUT-TO-HUT FROM WEST TO EAST

Route: St. Anton - Konstanzer Hut (Cat. I) - Darmstädter Hut (Cat. I) - Niederelbe Hut (Cat. I) - Edmund Graf Hut (Cat. I) - Pettneu. There is a motorable road to the Konstanzer Hut but only those with special passes, such as the Constance Section of the Alpenverein, may drive up it. Walkers from St. Anton can avoid the first kilometre or two of road and add a feature to the walk by starting up the Rosannaschlucht - a narrow gorge through which the River Rosanna flows after coming down from its source in the heart of the Ferwall and before passing through St. Anton to flow away down the Stanzertal towards Landeck. This is the slightly shorter way, but the guidebook, surprisingly, does not think it scenically as rewarding guidebook, surprisingly, does not think it scenically as rewarding as starting on the road, which also passes the chapel at Stiegeneck, with carved wooden figures worth seeing. After the 'Schlucht' the Gasthaus Ferwall offers an early opportunity for refreshment, and after a further hour through the forest the Wagner Hut, 1446m, offers yet another. The route presents no problems, and just before we reach the Vordere Branntwein Hut (but don't let its name, the Brandy Hut, raise your hopes for a schnapps!) the elegant spire of Patteriol soars up before us. This beautiful mountain, 3059m will dominate our stay at the Konstanzer Hut. but it is not a walker's mountain! Then over a bridge and up to the hut . Opened in 1885 and lying at 1765m this is a friendly and sociable hut, particularly when members of the Constance Section are in residence. (From St. Anton, about 3hrs.) Since this was written the Konstanzer Hut has been partly destroyed by an avalanche, but was rebuilt 1989-90.

Next morning's route (the Darmstädter Hut, 2384m, via the Kuchenjoch 2739), starts almost due south in the Fasultal through pine-woods. After crossing the first stream from the east the path begins to climb towards the east, at first through more woods and then in curves to gentle pasture-slopes; south-east to the cwm below the Kuchenloch, and east up to this (3hrs) Looking back we see Patteriol straight across the valley of the Fasulbach towering gigantically up, crowned with the horns of its doubly pointed summit.

The ascent of the Scheibler, 2988m from the Kuchenjoch must not be missed as the panoramic views from it are the most tremendous in the whole Ferwall. The route up the south ridge is obvious, well made and exciting The summit is small and rocky. Due south rises darkly the north face of the Kuchenspitze topped by its serrated summit ridge. South-west, Patteriol no longer fills the whole scene, for beyond it the southern ranges of the Ferwall are backed by the snows and glaciers of the Silvretta. The view north-east is more purely a rock landscape; the Scheibler's neighbour, the Faselfad Spitze, 2997m, an uncompromising stickleback of a mountain is only the foremost of a whole series of jagged rock peaks even as far as the Parseier Spitze in the Lechtal Alps. Almost exactly due east the Darmstädter Hut (2384m) is already clearly to be seen against its backdrop of peaks, the highest of them being the Saumspitz, 3034m.

Hoppe-Seyler Weg

The descent from the Kuchenjoch involves going steeply down the Kuchenferner (Kuchen Glacier) and an ice-axe may be useful. It is vital to keep well to the left to avoid crevasses. After the glaciated section the so-called Apotheke Way leads left of a minute tarn and so down to the hut. (About 4hrs from the Konstanzer Hut, *not counting the ascent of the Scheibler.*)

The Darmstädter Hut is magnificently placed with superb mountains all round, the highlight being the ice-fall of the Küchel Glacier between the Küchel Spitze (3148m) and the equally high Kuchen Spitze. The hut can suffer from severe water-shortage in dry weather.

The next day's walk to the Niederelbe Hut on the Hoppe-Seyler Way is the finest hut-link of this outing. First, a great arc below the Küchel Ferner, then, after climbing some way, a magnificent rock path across a rock buttress. After this, moraines and small snowfields to the Schneidjöchl (2841m): from here a splendid view of the Küchelferner and its attendant peaks. Steeply down the east side, losing nearly 300m altitude, then rambling on until the Hoppe-Seyler Way sets off dramatically across and up a cliff-face, rather in the manner of Jack's Rake plus rough steps, above which it zig-zags up to the delightful little, unwardened, open Kieler Hut at 2800m (Cat. I) - emergency accommodation for 14, with bunks, stove and even firewood and matches.

It is a long way down from here to the Niederelbe Hut at 2340m, and not altogether easy, crossing a very steep slope intersected by snow-filled gullies where stone-fall can be a hazard. When I visited this hut its elderly and toothless warden, Serafin Rudigier, gave the place a fine atmosphere with great good humour.

From the Niederelbe Hut you have the choice of two fine summits, the Madaunspitze (2960m) and the Kreuzjochspitze (2921m), both described as 'easy, very rewarding' in the German guidebook. Let us take the latter, - the 'Hut-Mountain' of the Niederelbe Hut. The ascent is easier than that of the Scheibler, but longer and more lonely. From the hut by its tarn, the Sess-see, go west for a while towards the Sessladjoch, but soon fork right (NW) and again after about $1/2$km take the right-hand track of three. (The middle one leads to the Madaunspitze.) At about 2650m we pass on the left of the Schwarz See - it *can* look very black - lying below scree

Hohe Riffler

rather as Goat's Water lies under Dow Crag. The south ridge of the Kreuzjochspitze is an easy rock scramble. A degree of route-finding ability is needed for this mountain, and you may well be on your own. The panorama from the inevitable summit cross is as wild as one could wish and as rewarding as promised in the book.

Any spare time at the hut may be used to stroll for half an hour as far as the Kappler Kopf (2407m) with its impressive views into the Paznauntal and across it to the Silvretta.

To continue the hut-to-hut route we take the Kieler Way. Its name, like that of the Kieler (Kiel) and Niederelbe (Lower Elbe) huts indicates the fact that the Alpine Club Section concerned with this area belongs to Schleswig-Holstein! The path starts due north but soon contours east along the Sessladalpe. After about 1km of this, fork north: the continuation east and downhill leads to the Alpine Guesthouse Dias, above Kappl. The Kieler Way continues, changing its name to the Riffler Way and climbing almost due north to the Schmalzgruben-Scharte. (According to the Kompass Wanderkarte the Riffler Way leads up to the Scharte which lies, so the map says at 2679m. According to Franz Malcher's guidebook the Scharte lies at about 2650m, which seems more probable, and the path changes its name here and not sooner - which again seems better sense.) The Schmalzgruben-Scharte is blessed with a fine stone 'man' and extensive views to the Lechtaler and Ötzaler Alps. After the easy ascent to this pass the descent is more dramatic, down a cwm called 'In der Schmalzgrube', across a ridge to the Schmalzgrubensee - a beautiful little lake cupped in rock and reflecting the majestic Riffler group - and then crossing a further ridge and down in zig-zags below a little glacier to the Edmund Graf Hut at 2375m.

This hut, which celebrated its centenary in 1985, was enlarged in 1973 and my wife and I were obviously the first to use our bedroom, which struck us as more like a hotel room! The hut is beautifully situated and possesses an open-air altar in a simple setting of stone and wood. It is very charming when the priest comes up from the valley to celebrate mass and imparts to the scene a religious quality that is perhaps not totally unlike the quality given to the Himalayas by the high Buddhist monasteries and chortens.

There are no real difficulties in climbing the Hohe Riffler (3162m) from the hut, at least to the south summit. There is a summit-book here, but the north summit and its cross (higher by a couple of metres) demands a bit of Grade II climbing. I am told with the retreat of the glaciers this has become easier. Much of the ascent is on loose scree, uncomfortable in descent, but the final crossing of the top edge of the steep and impressive Pettneuer Glacier between the Kleiner and Hoher Riffler, is a worthy finish. (The ascent takes about $2^{1/4}$hrs.)

From this summit we can look back over our route of the previous days: every summit we have visited is in sight. The downward views of glacier and rock are magnificent and dramatic, a fitting climax to the whole walk.

The path from the Edmund Graf Hut down the Malfontal to Pettneu presents no problems, and there are trains from there back to St. Anton if necessary.   (1973)

2. ROUND THE PATTERIOL GROUP

Route: Konstanzer Hut (Cat. I) - (Neue) Heilbronner Hut (Cat. I) - Friedrichshafener Hut (Cat. I) - Konstanzer Hut.

From the Konstanzer Hut (see Ferwall Walk 1 for approach) the more rewarding route to the Heilbronner Hut is by the Bruckmann Way over the Wannenjöchl (2684m), book time 5hrs, but if the weather is inclement - as it was when I did this route - we are better following the lower paths. This means walking north, then bearing west into the Schönferwalltal on the west side of the Patteriol group. A straightforward path by the Rosanna passes two alm huts, the Frasch Hut at 1822m and the Schönverwall Hut at 2007m. About 1km beyond this the Albona Bach joins the Rosanna from our right. Follow this up to the Scheidseen, twin lakes, or rather tarns, at 2270m, just beyond which is the Neue Heilbronner Hut at 2320m on the Verbellner Winterjöchl, one of the Ferwall watersheds. The hut lies pleasantly on green pastures, but the real quality of the site is created by the Scheid Lakes in which Patteriol and her associates are wonderfully reflected. From this angle Patteriol takes on a new aspect and one can see where the Bruckner Way comes over the Wannenjöchl. The lower route, by which we have come, passes through quite densely inhabited marmot country. (From the Konstanzer Hut via the Schonferwalltal $3^{1/2}$hrs.)

If the first day's walking was in every sense somewhat

pedestrian, the second more than compensates for any lack of drama. The Friedrichshafener Way climbs at first east-north-east over rather barren, stony country - though still with fine views, especially to the north and north-east - and rounding the northern end of the Jöchli Grat it turns south-east and, dropping but very little, goes into the upper part of the Ochsental where it crosses the Rosanna only a few hundred metres from its source. The path then climbs steeply to the Mutten Joch at 2660m (2hrs from the hut). So far the route has been bare and lonely, with little to relieve the sepia tones of rock and poor grasses. But at the Mutten Joch an opportunity occurs to achieve without difficulty a most rewarding viewpoint, the Geiss Spitze 2779m only 20mins from the pass. It is quite a scramble at the end and you may like to leave your rucksack part way up, but the views are quite extraordinary. To the north rise the sharp ridges of the Patteriol group, to the south the Jamtal, deep and remote, leads the eye to the gleaming Jamtal Glacier and the three-thousanders of the Silvretta; to the south-west there is just a glimpse of the Silvretta Stausee backed by the Grosser Litzner and other giants; while just below are the naked tarns that constitute the sources of the Rosanna. We leave the little rocky top reluctantly, especially as the way to the hut is somewhat uninteresting. When we walked it (1973) there was all the ugliness of a new road being built to the hut; now there is doubtless the ugliness of the road itself!

The Friedrichshafener Hut (2151m) was taken over by the Alpenverein from private ownership in 1924. It was quite a small hut in 1973 but has since been considerably enlarged. It stands by a little lake and overlooks the Paznauntal. From it one can still see the Geiss Spitze and recall those great views.

The return from this hut to the Konstanzer Hut over the Schafbuhel Joch (2636m) is straightforward and if pushed you can carry straight on back to St. Anton - about 24km altogether.
(1973)

(There are, of course, other walking possibilities in the group, but the only other hut of real walking importance is the Wormser Hut, and this is an 8-9hr walk from the next hut, the Neue Heilbronner. The route, however, is said to be scenically very rewarding.)

XIII: *The Ötztal Alps*
(AVE Group 30)

The so-called Ötztal Alps cover a vast area, far larger than the name implies:

Boundaries: The R. Inn from Landeck to its junction with the Ötztaler Ache; up the Ötztal as far as Zwieselstein; the Gurgler Ache to its junction with the Timmelsbach; up the Timmelsbach to the Timmelsjoch; over to the Schönauer Alm; down the Passeiertal to Merano (Meran); along the R. Adige (Etschtal) up to the Reschenpass, down to Finstermunz; then down the Inn back to Landeck.

This enormous area is subdivided into nine distinct groups. Of these we shall here be concerned with only four: the Hauptkamm (including the Hochwilde), the Weisskamm (including the Wildspitze), the Geigenkamm (including the Hohe Geige) and the Kaunergrat, but we shall define our walks in terms of the *approach valleys* used, viz. the Pitztal and the Ötztal, rather than by the actual mountain groups.

THE PITZTAL

The Pitztal is a long, deep, narrow valley running into the mountains due south of Imst - a good base for the motorised mountaineer. The valley was a 'late developer' as far as the ski-circus is concerned. But the valley head is now developed for summer skiing. On its west side rises the Kaunergrat with such fine climbers' mountains as the Verpeil Spitze and the Waze; on its east the Geigenkamm dominated by the Hohe Geige (3395m); at its southern end rise the great Taschach and Mittelberg Glaciers leading up to the glories of the Wildspitze (3770m) and its attendant courtiers. For the non-motorised there are buses as far as Mittelberg at the head of the valley road.

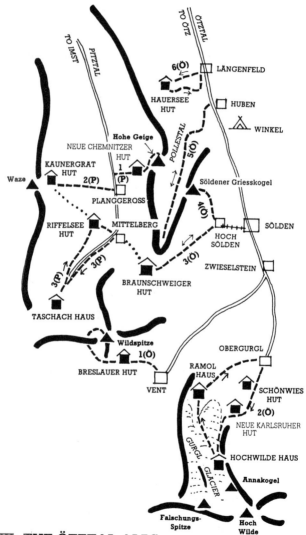

XIII: THE ÖTZTAL ALPS

1. THE HOHE GEIGE (3395m) (Using the Neue Chemnitzer Hut, 2323m (Cat. I)).

This is a most rewarding mountain, the highest in the Geigenkamm, but not at all difficult. It can involve snow, so an ice-axe may be useful; but though the mountain has three glaciers, none has to be crossed to reach the summit. A rope is not essential but may give confidence.

The path to the hut begins on the road at 1560m, about ³/₄km north of the hamlet of Planggeross (1617m): there are guest-houses here. If motorised you can park just where the path begins, and you can already see the hut, 2km away and 800m up, with its picturesque little corner turret. But the steep path is beautifully zig-zagged, and the time given on the signpost (2hrs 5mins) is extraordinarily accurate. There may be a pile of dry logs not far up the path with a notice asking you to carry one up. If so, do please play the game!

The path is charming, with foreground interest in the crags on one's left and the cascades of the stream on the right. Below is the valley with its now toy-size houses, and across the valley the Waze with its gleaming glaciers gradually comes into view.

The hut is small, friendly, and inconvenient! The Chemnitz section lost its original hut (now the Nevesejoch Hut) to Italy in 1922 and opened this 'new' one in 1926. To its west the view is magnificent, straight across the Pitztal into the hanging valley of the Planggeross Tal with the Waze (Watzespitze) and the Verpeil Spitze towering up beyond it. It is *possible* to 'do' the Hohe Geige and descend again to the valley all in one day, but to stay the night in the hut gives leisure for more enjoyment both of the mountain and of the situation of the hut.

The marked path to the Hohe Geige goes east into a big, rather ugly moraine basin and heads towards the Weiss Ferner, the small, steep glacier lying below the Amperkogel (3186m) whose rocky summit looks like a tower on a huge knoll - a sort of alpine Glastonbury Tor. At a fork, with sign, go left. (N.B. You must *pass* the last grassy ridge running down on your left and then circle back on to it, where there is a good zig-zag path.) Above the grassy ridge there is a rock ridge (note the red waymarks, and don't go up the loose scree-gully) a little on your right: it is easy. Make height on this. Then comes a fairly exposed traverse to the right and finally permanent snow and block-scree to the summit cross - with book.

Excellent views in all directions enhanced by the Geige's own glaciers as foreground. Return by same route. (The summit is 3-3$^{1/}$₂hrs from the hut.)   (1969)

2. THE KAUNERGRAT HUT (2860m) (Cat. I)

British walkers, as well as climbers, should visit this hut, as it is one to which the 'Sektion England' (now re-christened 'Sektion Britannia' in deference to its many Celtic members) of the AAC has contributed: in fact one of its bedrooms is called the 'British Room'.

The ascent begins at Planggeross, and if you are fortunate you may be able to send your bag up the first steep section on the *Materialseilbahn*. (We were *not* fortunate: the dialect-speaking man in charge alleged that with any more weight the Seilbahn would be *kaputt*.) Provisioning this hut is not easy. From the top of this ropeway a pony carries the goods (but not rucksacks) to a second ropeway. This latter has to be dismantled each season because of avalanches. The first section is picturesque, partly wooded and partly near the cascades of the Ludd-Bach. There are fine glimpses, too, of the head of the Pitztal, where the Linker Ferner Kogel can be spotted beyond the - invisible - Braunschweiger Hut. If you are still lumbered with your rucksack and the pony is below you, you may leave your bag in faith at the bottom of the second ropeway before tackling the final 300m of ascent up to the hut (2860m). About 4$^{1/}$₂hrs from Planggeross.

The hut is sure to be full of climbers aiming at the Waze or the Verpeilspitze. It is with real regret that I must omit the Waze (the highest peak of the Kaunergrat) from this book. The East Ridge up, followed by the glacier descent is as fine a mountain day as I have known, and our ascent in August 1969 was a modest celebration of the first ascent in September 1869 by Alois Ennnemoser, a local guide, at the instigation of Franz Senn. But Grade III climbing cannot fairly be called 'walking'!

(Unfortunately, neither of the continuations from the Kaunergrat Hut is easy. The crossing to the Verpeil Hut is only for the experienced, or with a guide. The 'Cottbuser Höhenweg' to the Riffelsee Hut is again recommended only to experienced mountaineers and suffers a good deal of stone-fall. So for most walkers the Kaunergrat Hut, in its superb mountain setting, must be an end in itself.)   (1969)

3.   THE TASCHACH HAUS (2434m) THE FULDAER WAY AND THE RIFFELSEE HUT (2293m)

At the very head of Pitztal, the end of the bus route and of the road, and with plenty of parking space (not free!) lies Mittelberg at 1740m, the remotest settlement in the valley inhabited all the year round. It is the Pitztal base for the Braunschweiger Hut and the glaciers and snow peaks beyond. The present walk is a modest one, taking two unhurried days, but outstanding in its scenic rewards. Summer skiing developments have, however, changed the character of the valley-head.

The actual path from Mittelberg is not particularly exciting and has been made passable for motor vehicles for part of the way; but it is enjoyable, with views of the snow-peaks ahead towards the south and of the Pitztal mountains - notably the Hohe Geige - to the north. The hut cable-way may sometimes take rucksacks from the end of the drivable track. The original Taschach *Hut* - still there and in use as a winter-room - was opened in 1874, being the third German mountain hut to be built in Austria. The Taschach *Haus* was built alongside in 1898-99 by the Frankfurt-am-Main section of the Alpine Club. It was further extended in the 1960s on an 'open-plan' system that ensures that the maximum volume of downstairs noise reaches the sleeping-quarters. It lies on the grassy tongue that leads down from the Pitztaler Urkund, which divides the Taschach Glacier on the east from the Sexegerten Glacier on the west. Even now, in the late 20th century, the Taschach Glacier and its ice-fall present an awe-inspiring 'lunar landscape', especially from viewpoints somewhat above the hut, but in the 18th and 19th centuries, when the glaciers were still advancing, an annual service of intercession was held at a pulpit hewn out of the ice, not indeed of this glacier but of the Mittelberg Glacier at the head of the other branch of the valley. Such was the peril in which the valley dwellers lived not so many decades ago.

The hut is the base for many ambitious expeditions in the Wildspitze and Hochvernagt groups, but we, after doubtless spending time admiring and photographing the glacier from those good viewpoints above the hut, are taking next morning the high level Fuldaer Way to the Riffelsee Hut, the next hut on the west side of the valley, just above Mittelberg - a mere 2¹/₂ to 3hrs. (Do not use after heavy snow. There is a less interesting, older, lower route as an alternative.) This path was opened in 1960, having been built by contractors with the help of an Alpine club youth group and others. There are no real difficulties - the odd fixed rope and snow patch - but the views NE including the Hohe Geige, and SE to the Wildspitze, magnificently towering above and beyond the glaciers, are among the Pitztal's finest. At one point an alcove between two boulders has been designated 'O O' (null null) by some alpine wit - an Austrian euphemism for W.C. After finally crossing the outflow of the lake - the Riffelsee - climb a slope to the hut: it will probably be full of noisy day-trippers. It is worthwhile to walk to the lake, a pretty tarn, before facing the descent of the steep, stony, eroded path, an outsize Rossett Gill, back to Mittelberg.   (1969)

(There is also a chair-lift $^{1/}$4hr from the hut, down to Mandarfen.)

THE ÖTZTAL

The Ötztal runs parallel with and to the east of the Pitztal, but is more extensive and varied, and moreover at 60km the longest of the Inntal's side valleys. In its lower (northern) reaches it is broad and fertile. Here lie the village resorts of Ötz (also written Oetz), Umhausen, Längenfeld and Huben - and other smaller ones. Längenfeld is celebrated as the birthplace of Franz Senn (1831-1884), the 'Glacier-Priest', one of the co-founders of the Austrian Alpine Club. Above Huben the valley narrows quite dramatically: there is an excellent campsite in this narrow section at Winkel. Above this, where the valley is again wider, lies Sölden, with many hotels and guest-houses, and a campsite. Some 4kms above Sölden, at Zwieselstein, the valley forks: to the right (west) it becomes the Ventner Tal whose village, Vent, is the base for the Wildspitze - Weisskugel group; to the left (east) it leads to the Timmelsjoch (now a major crossing to Italy) and to Obergurgl, which at 1927m is the highest 'church village' in the eastern alps. Once 'out of this world', Obergurgl is now developed as an important ski resort, often able to offer snow when other resorts are bare of it. But its village character has been virtually destroyed.

Only the mountains west of the line Ötztal-Timmelsjoch lie within the Ötztal Alps. Walks to the east, even if approached through the Ötztal, will be found under **Stubai Alps.**

1. THE WILDSPITZE (3770m)

Sometimes known as the Ötztaler Wildspitze, this is the highest mountain in the Weisskamm, the Ötztal Alps and the North Tirol. The summit cross is on the South Summit. The North Summit is nominally 2m higher, but has become lower through melting of the snow-cover. Involving as it does, glacier work and the risk of crevasses, this is one of the most serious walks in this Guide, even though it is not difficult given good ice-conditions. Unguided parties must be roped and equipped to deal with snow and ice.

Start at Vent, where the Ventner Tal divides into the Rofental (west) and Niedertal (east). It is now possible to use a chair-lift to Stablein, saving $1^{1/4}$hrs of steep path on the way to the Breslauer Hut (2840m) (Cat. I). The rest of the walk is scenically rewarding, especially where it passes below the tongue of the Rofenkar Glacier. It runs more or less NW over meadows into the valley of the Rofenbach, then crosses the Rofenbach and zig-zags more steeply up to the hut.

For the mountain itself make an early start in the morning, taking your cue from the guides! A well-marked path - for this is one of the most visited summits in the country - leads NW from the hut, rounding the S and SW spurs of the Wildspitze up the Mitterkar Glacier to its innermost 'bay'. Then aim N for the lowest point between the Wildspitze and the Hinterer Brochkogel: that is the Mitterkarjoch. Beware of a crevasse (Randkluft) which often forms here - and look out for it when coming down! - and climb steep snow to the joch. From here almost level, NE into the basin of permanent snow, then up the middle of this (beware crevasses!) to a more level section. Bear right (south) looking out for crevasses, and climb the steep final snow ridge (often iced!) to the summit cross (South Summit). The views - weather permitting - such as one expects from the highest mountain in the area.

Return by the same route, with particular care for crevasses of the 'Bergschrund' type across your route: keep roped up for safety. Remember snow will be softer than it was earlier in the morning. Avalanching does occur below the Mitterkarjoch. (1966)

2. A ROUND WALK ABOVE OBERGURGL (3 days minimum)

Obergurgl (1927m) - Skihütte Schönwies (2262m) (privately owned) - Neue Karlsruher Hütte (2438m Cat. I) - Hochwildehaus (2883m) (Cat. I) - Ramolhaus (3006m) (Cat. I) - Obergurgl

Summits from the Hochwildehaus (add one day for each): Hochwilde (or Hohe Wilde) North Summit (3461m); Falschungsspitze (3363m); Annakogel (3336m).

This is one of Walter Pause's 100 Best Walks in the Alps and he rightly describes parts of it as 'unforgettable'. The straight walk to the Hochwildehaus and back - well worthwhile for its own sake - can be undertaken by any competent mountain walker, but the rest involves glacier crossings and must only be attempted by properly equipped, roped parties.

Leave Obergurgl up a pack-pony track following at first the line of the Gaissberg chair-lift. In the ski-season the traffic-jammed Gaissberg is the worry of all beginners, who must finish down this after spending the day on easier nursery slopes above it. Cross the miniature gorge of the Gaissberg Bach and continue south into the Rotmoostal. In front, the Hangerer (3021m) raises its grim cliffs. With the Schönwies Hut in sight, cross the Rotmoos Ache on a footbridge. To your left is a great view up the Rotmoostal, at whose head towers the Heuflerkogel (3245m) and its attendant peaks. The Schönwies is so beautifully sited that you may well pause here for drinks. The hut is primarily intended for skiers, and even beginners capable only of a 'blue' route can enjoy a crowded lunch-time here in the winter. After the hut, the path crosses a boggy area and re-enters the valley of the Gurgler Ache, rising gently, high above its great gorge. Pass the Gurgler Alm Hut and a further isolated building which promises to be the next hut, but isn't, and finally drop a little to the Neue Karlsruher Hütte (2438m) now known as the Langtalerleck Hut. After 2¹/₂hrs walking from Obergurgl you will have earned your lunch.

This is an elegant hut in a magnificent situation overlooking the great ice-fall of the Gurgl Glacier - a mighty 'fossilised waterfall'. The pony track ends here and a goods ropeway soars crazily across a tributary valley and high up the precipices at the north end of the Schwarzenkamm - up which the path also goes, after descending sharply into the gorge of the tributary stream, which it crosses on a swaying 'Tibetan' bridge. The ascent of the cliff is of course nothing like as steep as it appears and the only really exposed corner is protected by a fixed rope. A fine section of path! But it is also good to emerge on to the side of the Schwarzenkamm with the Gurgl

Glacier on one's right, the 'Ramol' peaks to the NW, with the Ramolhaus (3006m) perched incredibly high aloft.

A straight tramp due south, climbing gently, leads to the now visible Hochwildehaus (2883m). The hut stands on what is aptly called the Stone Table (am steinernen Tisch) and enjoys a situation second to none in the area, only yards from the edge of the glacier, which rises towards a vista of rock and snow peaks - the Hochwilde Annakogel, Mitterkamm and Falschungsspitze - to name only the most obvious. Whether this hut is your final goal or not, drink in this memorable scene.

It is best to have checked at Obergurgl that the hut is open and wardened, for there have been problems about wardenship at times in the past. Also, during the Austro-Italian border dispute concerning the South Tirol back in the 1960s strange things seemed to happen here. The warden, instead of endlessly and unmusically strumming some sort of guitar might unexpectedly go outside at 10p.m. to sound 'The Last Post' on a bugle: impressive, but odd! Or a climber going down to the loo at midnight might surprise a party equipped for departure who flashed torches and scuttled away. But today the distant gunfire is no longer heard and the border dispute has long been settled

Here follow descriptions of three summit ascents possible from the Hochwildehaus. In normal conditions none of them presents real difficulties, but they are all serious through altitude and situation and they all involve glacier-crossing and its appropriate skills. The top of the Hochwilde involves rock-climbing and exposure. (A guide will almost certainly be available at the hut if required.)

A. Hochwilde (Hohe Wilde) North Summit (3461m)

Allow $3^{1/}2$-4 hours for the ascent from the hut. A desperately early start is not needed - 5 or 5.30a.m. in August, when the alpenglow is touching the tops with rose. Roped for safety it is easy to cross the glacier on the 'trade route' (so long as visibility is good) to the Annajoch (3150m) between the Annakogel and the Mitterkamm: about 2hrs. Then bear left, keeping SW of the Annakogel, up the snow-slope to the snow-ridge of the Hochwilde. This leads to the first gendarme. Its crossing is graded II, but the 'steps' have evidently been artificially enlarged and there is a fixed wire rope.

From this there is a short descent; then an exposed traverse on the east side of the ridge, soon leading up to the North Summit. This traverse, though not technically difficult, is quite dramatic in its exposure and some of the footholds are supplied by iron spikes driven into the rock: to be taken seriously. The views into Italy and Austria are stupendous. (Dominating the view to the SE, the South Summit, 21m higher, looks tempting. The jagged ridge between the two summits, the so-called 'Gustav-Becker-Way' gives rock/snow 'scrambling', with protection in places. It is for experienced climbers and not included in this guidebook.)

The descent - by the same route - will probably take only a couple of hours to the hut. The first ascent was made in 1871. Bear in mind that in adverse conditions this mountain can quickly become both difficult and dangerous, and that mist and/or snow can make route-finding on the glacier a serious problem. If in doubt when setting out, speak to the hut warden.

B. Falschungsspitze (3363m)
(Allow 3¹/₂hrs ascent from the hut)
Start the glacier crossing at the same point as for the Annajoch, but head roughly SSW, aiming for the right-hand (north) end of the Mitterkamm. Passing this continue S, then SW then S again. The Falschungsspitze is the summit of the right (west) of two rock spurs running down from the main ridge. (The other, 54m lower, is the Bankkogel.) The easy route climbs the snow slope W and SW of the spur, running SE direct to the summit. No difficulties: the usual rules for glacier-crossing. The rock ridge can be climbed direct and though the rock is rather loose, if the bottom section is avoided by using snow, nothing harder than 'Difficult' will be found. In any case, use the snow slope for the return.

C. Annakogel (3336m)
(Allow at least 3hrs from the hut)
From the Hochwildehaus the Annakogel looks like a symmetrical snow dome with a little rock 'nipple' on its summit. In fact it is a rock summit formed at the junction of the south end of the Schwarzenkamm with the continuation of the Mitterkamm ridge SE of the Annajoch. Start as for the Hochwilde - i.e. keeping close to

the Schwarzenkamm on the east of the glacier, but as it steepens below the Annajoch do not bear right but continue almost due south. Permanent snow leads almost the whole way (as promised by the view from the hut) but there is easy rock near the summit. This is the easiest and shortest of the three summit ascents described here. (The Mitterkamm is not recommended here. It is a rock climb rather than a walk, and some of the rock is very brittle and unsound.)

The Round Walk continued

From the Hochwildehaus follow the original approach path for 500m or so. At its nearest point to the glacier, step on to the glacier and go NW. When nearly across, bear N and so pick up the continuation of the path to the Ramol Haus at the far side. Do not go too far W or N on the glacier or you will meet bad crevasses. Follow the AAC map indication and you will probably find the crevasses impacted. But rope up and take all normal precautions. On the far side it is a steep climb to the Ramol Haus. If you are short of a day, there is a branch track NNE soon after leaving the glacier which goes straight back to Obergurgl, picking up the path from the Ramol Haus. The Ramol Haus, however, is worth a visit and the path thence down the west side of the valley whose east we ascended to reach the Hochwildehaus, is rewarding. (1966)

3. THE BRAUNSCHWEIGER HUT (2759m Cat. I)

Although the Braunschweiger Hut belongs to the Pitztal and is most conveniently reached from Mittelberg at the head of that valley, it is the goal for an interesting walk from the Ötztal. It is the base hut for several not difficult summits (but involving glacier crossings), and the descent from it to Mittelberg, though steep in parts, is not problematical.

Only masochists now struggle from Sölden itself: bulldozing for ski-piste has long since made the route miserable. Drive to Hochsölden - 20mins in low gear - or take the lift. You can walk from here or take a further lift to the Rotkogelhang at 2400m. A good track leads on to the slope of the (true) left of the Rettenbachtal. Then the path goes up barren moraines, keeping to the right of the Rettenbach Ferner (Glacier) and finally up a steep field of permanent snow to the dramatic Pitztaler Jöchl. You can see the hut from here but follow the waymarks with care. Keep left (south) on the

'Karlesschneide' and then down to the hut in zig-zags. The protection on the old route round the north of the corrie no longer exists and there is a 30m rock step to cope with!

The hut is large and magnificently situated on a rocky knob above the Karlesferner, and was built in 1892. Worth a visit! (1966)

4. THE SÖLDENER GRIESSKOGEL (2811m)

This makes an easy half-day outing of about 5hrs in all from Hochsölden - reached by car or lift.

The walk begins dully enough up broad bare slopes scarred and bulldozed for skiing, but after these it becomes a good traverse path and finally steep and dramatic up the SE flank to the summit. The summit is not particularly pronounced but this is well compensated for by the fact that it forms part of the jagged and rocky mountain ridge which separates the Ötztal from the branch valley, the Pollestal (see Walk 5), and whose almost Cuillin-like silhouette provides a theatrical foreground for views which extend in the south to the glaciers and peaks of the Wildspitze group and in the west across the Geigenkamm to the Kaunergrat, where the Waze rises above everything. The Pollestal lies deep below. It is a particularly rewarding viewpoint to visit for an easy day after more ambitious walks have made the whole area somewhat familiar. (1971)

5. THE POLLESTAL

The Pollestal is a wild, lonely hanging valley some 10km long, running from the Ötztal just south of Huben to the Pollesjoch (2961m) close to the Pitztaler Joch above the Braunschweiger Hut. It is an old but now little-used crossing from Ötztal to Pitztal either by the Pollesjoch to the Braunschweiger Hut and Mittelberg, or by the Weissmaurachjoch (2923m) to the Neue Chemnitzer Hut and Planggeross. Both the passes require more alpine experience than the Pitztaler Joch, and are not described here. However, this 'Lost Valley', which is rather like Glen Nevis on a large scale, is worth a visit in its own right. It is the valley that can be seen far below the Söldener Griesskogel (Walk 4).

Walk south from Huben village across meadows and cross the 'old river' (no longer the main course of the Ötztaler Ache) by a bridge. Enter a little valley to the west of a wooded hill, Eck (1607m), and walk up in the woods on a good path to a saddle. ('Sattel' on map) at 1501m. Just about when passing a little shrine with a seat near it you swing south-west into the Pollestal, just at the head of its precipitous gorge. This gorge, which is what the path has evaded, debouches into the Ötztal just opposite the Winkel campsite, from which it is an impressive feature of the view.

Up the valley, keeping the stream, the Pollesbach, on your left, as far as the Vorderer (or 'Ausserer') Polles Alm (1773m). The path crosses the stream here. Don't fail to appreciate views across the Ötztal to the Stubai Alps before entering the wilder, barer, stonier and altogether more Scottish reach of the valley that follows - now running SSW. Even here the austerity is broken here and there by natural alpine gardens. On the left is the rugged ridge that is dominated by the Söldener Griesskogel, on the right are the steep slopes of the Geigenkamm.

How far you go is a matter for you, for unless you have an experienced party you should not attempt either joch towards the Pitztal. The Innerer Pollesalm (2083m - i.e 310m higher than the 'Vorderer': do not underestimate this valley!) is as far beyond the 'Vorderer' as that is beyond the shrine and seat. As far above again, the route over the Haimbach Jöchl (2727m) comes over from Hochsölden: this is also only for the experienced and makes demands on route-finding ability. Even before reaching the Innerer Pollesalm you will glimpse the valley-head and the small Polles Glacier looking very remote and some 800m higher than the alm. To reach the actual joch involves an ice-field, and the crossing into the Pitztal is not easy. It is not described here. Turn back when time or other factors dictate. The return walk is as delightful as the walk up. Keep to the path: the gorge is dangerous. (1971)

6. THE HAUERSEE (2331m) FROM LÄNGENFELD

The Hauersee is a beautiful, tarn-like lake lying in the Luibiskar, a wild and lovely spot that has been described as 'Coire Lagan plus a glacier'. Above it rise the serrated peaks of the Geigenkamm, with three tops of over 3000m - the Luibiskogel (3112m), the Reiserkogel (3090m) and the Hauerseekogel (3059m). There are serious high-level routes from here to the Frischmann Hut to the north (4hrs) and to the Neue Chemnitzer Hut on the Pitztal side (7hrs!). Primarily to link those two huts a hut was built here in 1928-9 by the Jung-Leipzig section of the Alpine Club, but this was later destroyed by

123

an avalanche. Between 1964 and 1969 a tiny new hut was built (to sleep 8 at most). It is a 'self-cooker', unwardened and requiring a special key from the warden of one of the other two huts. But the walk suggested here is simply a day-visit for the sake of the superb scenery and situation.

Start from Oberried. The path is steep and rough, with cat-walks in places, which may well have been repaired since the new hut was built. The route follows the stream which in fact issues from the Hauersee itself. It is a walk of great beauty, and after the destruction of the old hut one met fragments of it 30mins before reaching the site. In 1966 the foundations of the old hut were to be seen and the beginning of the new, with piles of timber and other materials brought in by helicopter. Like a Cuillins corrie, the Luibiskar gains in impressiveness if there has been a skittering of snow on the scree and rock-peaks above.

To vary the return take a right fork across the stream below steep zig-zags and traverse on a path gradually falling in a broad curve on the northern slopes of the Hauerkogel (not to be confused with the Hauerseekogel). Then drop down through forest to the Trinity Chapel, or Plague Chapel, a partly late-Gothic building dating from 1661, and so into Oberlängenfeld.

(N.B. The route from Oberried by the stream described here does not agree with the route given in the German guidebook and may therefore lack official approval. The route given in the German guidebook takes an alm-path to the Innerberg Alm and then continues on a broad spur. There is also a path from Unterried via the Innerberg Alm, and a longer route from Umhausen via Köfels, the Wurzberg Alm, Leck Alm and Innerberg Alm. Allow $3^{1}/2$hrs from Längenfeld, 4hrs from Umhausen.)

(1966. Further information 1982)

(Note: For the Venetberg, see The Lechtal Alps, Walk 9.)

XIV: The Stubai Alps
(AVE Group 31)

The Name: The Stubai Alps take their name from the largest, best known high valley within the group - the Stubai Valley. The name is first recorded in the year AD 1000, but probably goes back to pre-Roman times.

Boundaries of the Group: The R. Inn from the junction with the Ötztaler Ache to Innsbruck; up the R. Sill (the Wipptal) to the Brenner Pass, down the R. Eisack (Isarco) to Sterzing (Vipiteno); up the Jaufental (Valle del Giovo) to the Jaufen Pass (Passo del Giovo) and over this to St. Leonard (S. Leonardo); up the Passeiertal (Val Passiria) to the Schönauer Alm; over the Timmelsjoch, down the Timmelsbach to its junction with the Gurgler Ache; this becomes the Ötztaler Ache at Zwieselstein: down this to its junction with the R. Inn.

From the walker's viewpoint, this large area, like the Ötztal Alps, is best divided in terms of approach valleys. Those which concern the present selection of walks are:

A) The Nedertal-Obertal-Sellraintal

B) The Stubaital, with its subsidiaries the Pinnistal, Langental, Oberbergtal

C) The Ötztal, with the Sulztal and the Windachtal.

A. THE NEDERTAL - OBERTAL - SELLRAINTAL

This valley series links the Ötztal with Sellrain over the Kühtai Saddle (2016m), just below which lies Kühtai (1967m). The road is normally kept open all the year round, for Kühtai, although it boasts the old Hunting Lodge of Kaiser Maximilian, has been developed into a standard, packaged winter ski resort with most of its many hotels and guest-houses closed in summer. It also contains one of the Alpine Club's most luxurious and hotel-like huts, the Dortmunder Hut (1948m Cat. II), the base for the walks that follow. As this hut is easily reached by bus or in your car, advance booking is strongly recommended! The approach from the Ötztal, though

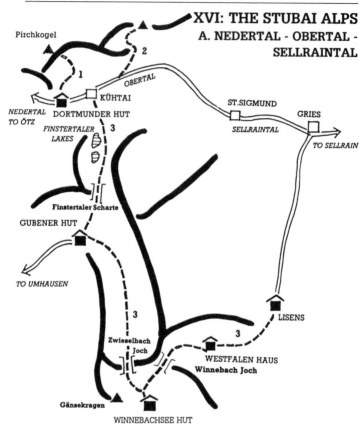

XVI: THE STUBAI ALPS
A. NEDERTAL - OBERTAL -
SELLRAINTAL

Pirchkogel

2

1

OBERTAL

KÜHTAI

ST.SIGMUND

GRIES

NEDERTAL
TO ÖTZ

DORTMUNDER HUT

SELLRAINTAL

TO SELLRAIN

FINSTERTALER
LAKES

3

Finstertaler Scharte

GUBENER HUT

TO UMHAUSEN

3

LISENS

3

Zwieselbach
Joch

WESTFALEN HAUS
Winnebach Joch

Gänsekragen

WINNEBACHSEE HUT

steeper, is shorter and will probably be found the most convenient for private motorists; but those using public services may prefer the Postbus from Gries-im-Sellrain to a private bus firm on the Ötztal side.

1. PIRCHKOGEL (2828m)

This fine mountain, 'Birchkogel' on some maps, reached in about 2¹/₂hrs from Kühtai, is a popular viewpoint - yet you may well have it to yourself. From the hut walk up into the 'village' and take the path north from the Silzer Hof Hotel. This begins steeply but soon leads to easier alpine pastures, the Stockacher Böden. These lead up to a great corrie, the Schwarzmoos, filled with massive boulders and a number of small and beautiful lakes. Here the path bears left, steeply up a ridge just north of the Hintere Griesskogel (2673m) - which can also be reached by this route. Finally a good and exciting ridge to the summit.

There is a fine panorama of Stubai Alps to the south, with a beautiful view into the Finster Tal in which nestle twin lakes. To the NE the foreground is dominated by the awesome Irzwände (2757m), a black cliff with shattered ridge - rarely climbed and as dangerous as it looks - above and beyond which towers the trapezium-shaped summit of the Rietzer Griesskogel (2884m). To the west the Nedertal drops away to the Ötztal, and the Inn Valley can be glimpsed. Return by same route. (1971)

2. RIETZER GRIESSKOGEL (2884m)

This mountain is apparently climbed chiefly from the huts on its northern side, the Peter Anich Hut and the Neuburger Hut, as an addition to the ascent of the slightly lower but more popular Hocheeder (2798m). But the ascent from the Kühtai side presents no technical difficulties, only navigational ones - unless the waymarks have been repainted.

From the Dortmunder Hut walk on the road up through Kühtai, over the pass and down the other side. The path, whose start may be tricky to find, begins in the area marked 'bei der Marche' on the AAC map and traverses the SE and E slopes of the K1. Mugkogel, with the Klamm Bach, in its miniature gorge, lying below to the walker's right. Eventually the path crosses the stream and climbs, with zig-zags, almost due north directly towards the Kreuzjochspitze (2750m). Look out for a fork, and take the right-hand path almost due east, soon bearing NE up a bare and stony slope called the Zirnbacher Narrenböden. Good views towards S - perhaps better appreciated on the return journey. Above the 'Narrenböden' (Fools' Ground) the path climbs steeply due north on to the upper part of the west ridge of the Griesskogel. Turn east and the summit is soon reached. Impressive views all round . Return same way. (1971)

3. ROUND TOUR OF NW STUBAI (3-4 Days) Dortmunder Hut (1948m Cat. II) - Finstertaler Scharte (2719m) - Guben-Schweinfurter Hut (2034m Cat. I) - Zwieselbach Joch (2870m) - Winnebachsee Hut (2362m Cat. I) - Winnebach Joch (2788m) - Westfalen Haus (2273m Cat. I) - Lisens (Lüsens) - Gries.

(Optional summit from Winnebachsee Hut: Gänsekragen (2915m))

This is one of the best round walks in the Stubai Alps, full of interest, variety and beauty, yet without serious difficulties.

The path starts SE from the hut, joins the Finstertal Bach and climbs in zig-zags to the first lake - Vorderer Finstertaler See (2240m). Enjoy the level walk beside this and then climb gently - only 18m! - to the second (Hinterer) lake. The whole valley, with its twin lakes, is most attractively picturesque. Beyond the second lake the path steepens through a great bare corrie - S then E, then S again up the west side of the corrie. Quite an effort at the top (2719m).

(From this pass, if you wish, you can without serious difficulty reach the summit of the Kraspesspitze (2953m) - but do not underestimate the additional time involved - probably over 1¹/2hrs.)

The descent to the Gubener Hut from the pass is easy: scree at first, then grass; steep towards the end. It is a most pleasant hut, quite different from the 'Hotel' feeling of the Dortmunder. You may even see one of the girls cleaning the spuds with a stiff yard-brush in a very alpine wooden trough outside. The hut lies at the head of the Horlachtal above Umhausen in the Ötztal and at the foot of the Zwieseltal - our next day's walk, a long, but beautiful ascent, SE at first, then bending gradually due south, the route being punctuated by some gracefully tapering 'stone men'. Towards the top avoid the Zwieselbach Glacier by keeping on the path well to its right. At the Zwieselbach Joch (2870m) a new world bursts upon the sight, dominated to the SW by the massive Breiter Griesskogel (3287m) almost wholly clothed in permanent snow (Firn).

(Although this summit can be reached from the Joch in about 1¹/2hrs, non-climbing walkers should not attempt it: at best it is only Grade I, but as the snow-cover diminishes over the years some sections, in certain conditions, can reach Grade III.)

Leaving this tempting summit to others therefore, we go down steep and unstable scree. Watch the red waymarks! An attempt to find an 'easier' way can soon waste an hour, if nothing worse. After

Totealp Hut, Rätikon
Piz Buin, Silvretta

Kleiner Riffler, Ferwall
Falschungspitze from Hochwilde Haus, Ötztal

this, the descent is good to the idyllically situated Winnebachsee Hut - small and friendly, too.

It is worth staying two nights at this hut in order to climb the Gänsekragen (2915m) - though why it should be called 'Geese-collar' is a mystery. It lies almost due west of the hut and the start of the ascent is deceptively easy, though it soon becomes very steep and but for a path constructed about 1912 would be very hard. Actually there are no serious problems and the tiny summit with cross and seat(!) is most dramatic, with views not only of nearby Stubai mountains, passes and valleys, but also away over to the giants of the Ötztal Alps, the Wildspitze (3772m) high above them all. (From hut to summit $1^{1}/_{2}$-2hrs.)

Also above the Winnebachsee Hut, to the east, you can walk up to a lovely little lake, ideal for a swim if the weather is hot.

Next morning, start due north from the hut retracing initially the path from the Zwieselbach Joch, but after a kilometre or less leave this and fork right - due north - on the path to the Winnebach Joch and the Westfalen Haus. This is a long and laborious ascent through a wilderness of boulders, the path often not well marked. At about 2600m the path swings NE and continues similarly near the lower edge of the Winnebach Glacier until the Winnebach Joch is thankfully reached at 2788m. Keep left of the minuscule glacier on the far side of the joch, then follow the path without difficulties almost due E down to the very fine Westfalen Haus (2273m). You may well reach this in time for lunch and then must consider whether to stay or press on. The path down to Lisens (or Lüsens) through the Längental is easy and pleasant. At Lisens there is a sizeable guest-house which since the 12th century has been the property of the Wilten Monastery. It seemed tatty and touristy to me and we did not stay - but it could have been improved. From Lisens, if you are lucky, you may catch a bus (perhaps disguised as a large car) down to Gries-im-Sellrain. The 2-$2^{1}/_{2}$hr walk down the road would be tedious. There are only private guest-houses in Gries and they *can* be booked out. You may well have missed the Postbus up the valley to Kühtai, and it's a long way. You may even have to use the Lisens 'bus' as a taxi - and there *may* be a bed for you in the Dortmunder Hut. We were lucky - there was one room for one night: perhaps you can plan less dicily! (1971)

B. THE STUBAI TAL

This valley, the largest and best-known of the high valleys in the group to which it gives its name, branches off the main valley of the Sill (which leads from Innsbruck to the Brenner Pass) 1km or so south of the Europa Bridge on the Brenner motorway. There is a good road the whole length of the valley to Ranalt (1260m) at its head; indeed you can now drive or catch a bus right up to the Mutterberg Alm at 1728m. From here it is now possible to go up to the Dresdner Hut (2302m Cat. II) by lift, and way up beyond it on the second section of the Stubaier Gletscherbahn to the Stubaier Eisjoch at 3133m. The 'development' is to promote downhill skiing, more profitable to the local community than mountain walking and climbing, and it cannot but be regretted by anyone who knew and valued the comparative isolation of the valley-head before.

On our return to the Stubai in 1990 I wrote: "The name 'Mutterberg *Alm*' is now a bitter mockery. There are three large, vulgar hotels plastered with commercial advertisements, several kiosks, three or four huge car parks with no attempt to soften their barren and rectangular impact, and the valley station of the cable-car, as big, ugly and inappropriate as a large railway station. Perhaps we should have taken photographs! People were snooty and rude, and we knew we were no longer with real mountain people. With difficulty we found the bus stop."

Nor do the locals all welcome the development. A Neustift shopkeeper exclaimed "Der Gletscher geht kaputt!" (The glacier is being destroyed) and explained that over-use was doing this by raising the temperature.

The Stubai Valley has three important tributary valleys. At Milders (1039m), where the main valley becomes the Unterbergtal, the Oberbergtal goes off to the NW, swinging round to SW almost parallel with the Unterbergtal. It leads up to Oberriss (1602m) above which the path continues to the Franz-Senn Hut (2147m Cat. I). Just above Ranalt the main valley again changes to the Mutterberger Tal, and the Langental branches due S to the Nürnberger Hut (2297m Cat. I). Further down the main valley, between Neustift and Medraz another major tributary, the Pinnistal, branches south. Up this is reached the Innsbrucker Hut (2369m Cat. I), the base for the ascent of Habicht (3277m).

There are two campsites in the valley, "Camping Stubai" in the middle of Neustift and "Camping Hochstubai" higher up the valley at an almost non-existent hamlet called Volderau.

1. ROUND THE HEAD OF THE STUBAI TAL

This is the Stubai Valley walk, and one of the most satisfying walks of its length in Austria.

The complete round comprises: Innsbrucker Hut (2369m Cat. I) - Bremer Hut (2413m Cat I) - Nürnberger Hut (2297m Cat. I) - Sulzenau Hut (2191m Cat. I) - Dresdner Hut (2302m Cat. II) - Neue Regensburger Hut (2286m Cat. I) - Franz-Senn Hut (2147m Cat. I) - Starkenberger Hut (2229m Cat. I)

XIV: THE STUBAI ALPS

B. STUBAI TAL

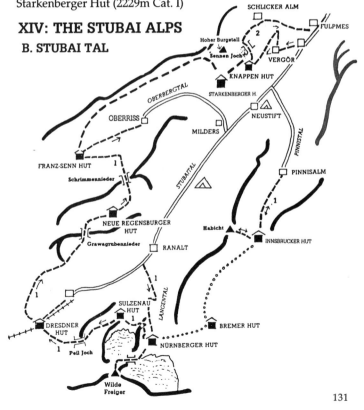

The Innsbrucker Hut (2369m Cat. I) and Habicht (3277m)

Unless you actually *enjoy* being engulfed in clouds of dust raised by jeeps filled with gaping tourists, do not walk up the Pinnistal from Neder, but join the tourists and take the jeep yourself up the valley to the Pinnisalm (1559m). If you think you are saving your fare by walking, you deceive yourself: you will spend as much on drinks at the Herzeben Alm *en route* if you walk!

Above the Pinnisalm you will walk free of the tourists and may even find that the Kar Alm (1737m) is open for refreshments. The path then climbs even more steeply in large curves to the Pinnisjoch (2369m) immediately beyond which is the large hut. (Considerable alterations were due to be made in 1982 and '83.) This is your base for Habicht (3277m) immediately behind the hut, the mountain which really dominates the head of the Pinnistal. It is grade I+, so do not attempt it unless you are good at scrambling. It was the first mountain in the Stubai to be climbed by a 'tourist', in 1836, probably by the route from the east described here. A path of sorts protected in places by wire ropes in various conditions leads fairly directly to the eastern corner of the summit massif. You must then cross the Habicht Glacier and may feel happier if you have an ice-axe. Then up easy rock to the summit. Be sure to return by exactly the same route! Many accidents occur because people cross the snowfield and take the steep snow gully to the left of the correct descent route: this breaks off suddenly over a cliff that falls into the Pinnistal. You have been warned!

(The next two sections of the round walk, Innsbrucker Hut to Bremer Hut and Bremer Hut to Nürnberger Hut are not easy and the former is long - 6 or 7hrs - into the bargain.)

To start at the **Nürnberger Hut** take the bus to Ranalt. From Ranalt walk up the Langental - steeply at first - to the B'such Alm. You should be able to get refreshment here and send your rucksack up the goods ropeway before tackling the next section on the west side of the valley, where zig-zags take you up about 400m in a bee-line distance of 1km. Above this the path still presses upward, nearly another 300m of height in about 1¹/₂km, through bleak country, very rocky all round, with rock and snow above. The hut when you reach it (about 3hrs from Ranalt) is a tall, impressive building - 3 storeys plus attics - built in 1886 and enlarged several

Nürnberger Hut

times. It has a spacious feeling about it. The guest-rooms are on the first, not the ground floor, and a strangely old-fashioned air is given by the drinking fountains on the landings. Though the 'Victorian' ones have now been replaced by more modern ones.

It is worth staying here a couple of nights in order to climb the **Wilde Freiger** (3418m Grade I. About 4hrs ascent). This is a snow summit: you will usually find that a top called 'Wild' is snow-covered and one called 'Aper' is of rock.

Follow the signposted and marked path south from the hut. It is well made and is built-up where necessary. It takes you easily up across the east face of the Urfall Spitz (2808m), then bears right (west) to the Seescharte (2762m). From the Seescharte the path continues SW. Keep to the northern edge of a small snowfield, to a rock ridge: up this, rather like an easy Crib Goch, with the Wilde Freiger Glacier plunging away to the right and the Grübl Glacier on your left. Finally up easy snow to the summit. The views are said to be magnificent. My own visit was cloudy at the top. (First ascent was 1869.) Return the same way. (NB. If you are prepared to carry all your gear up, you can go directly to the Sulzenau Hut from the

Wilde Feiger and glacier from nameless tarn

Seescharte without returning to the Nürnberger Hut but this route is *not* easy.)

There are two easier routes from the Nürnberger Hut to the Sulzenau Hut; the shorter, via the Niederl (2680m) demands surefootedness and a good head. The longer route crosses the ridge between the Niederl and the Mairspitze (2781m) - whose ascent can be an 'optional extra'. Both routes make the same start, but after about 10mins the Mairspitze route branches off to the north. It is a rambling agreeable path leading eventually to a rocky col with magnificent views of the Wilde Freiger. (It is from this point that the rock ridge to the right leads to the Mairspitze summit.) The descent on the far side is steep, with fine views of the Wilde Freiger and its attendant glacier, to a little tarn at 2552m where favourable conditions ought to provide photographers with a masterpiece. The easier continuation below leads to the Grünau See, an emerald lake set in a 'green meadow' that gives it its name. The Wilde Freiger Glacier (alternatively the Grünau Glacier) comes down towards it: perhaps the most beautiful spot you visit on this whole walk. From here easy and pleasant going among streams and moraines takes us to the

Sulzenau Hut (2191m). The hut the writer visited in 1968 was built in 1929, enlarged in 1939 and 1959, and destroyed in 1975. The present hut - large and interestingly designed - was built between 1976 and 1978. You may well decide to stay the night here, but if you are early in the day you can continue to the Dresdner Hut (2302m) Cat. II), but be warned that this very large and popular hut (80B, 100M) is reached by cable-car from the Mutterberg Alm and attracts *summer* skiers! The Sulzenau Hut (2191m Cat. I) has no artificial aids to access.

To approach it from the valley take the bus, which stops at the bottom of every hut path. Notice the Grawa waterfall as you pass in the bus. The path climbs steadily, and at first fairly shadily, up the south face of the valley until it gets above the great waterfall, then turns and follows the stream up into the vast rock basin that contains the Sulzenau Alm. This basin was under threat during the 1980s as the state railway wanted to dam it for a hydro-electric scheme. A well-planned zig-zag path takes you to the hut in about an hour. For good glacier photo opportunities without crossing a glacier try a walk up the Lübecker Way. Start as for the Peiljoch, then branch left to get on to the ridge of the lateral moraine near the Blaue Lacke (2289m)   (1990)

From the Sulzenau Hut the path leads up and along moraines, much of it indeed along the ridge of a fine lateral moraine, until a final pull up the well-made path brings you to the Peiljoch, a rocky pass at 2676m. The descent is, once more, steeper and less sound underfoot. The Dresdner Hut stands quite impressively on a spur below the Egesengrat (2653m), a viewpoint some 330m above the hut itself. The view of the Schaufelspitze (3333m) from here is particularly good.

(The Dresdner Hut is one of the best from which to climb the highest peak in the Stubai, the Zuckerhütl (3505m). It is not to be recommended to the inexperienced, though in good conditions it presents no problems to the experienced.)

The day's walk from the Dresdner Hut to the Neue Regensburger Hut (2286m) is the grandest of the round. Briefly, the path traverses the slopes high up on the NW side of the Mutterberger Tal until it crosses a high pass, the Grawagrubennieder (2880m) into a great hanging valley above the Falbesantal, a steep side-valley which leaves the main Unterbergtal at Falbesan.

Starting, surprisingly, due west, the route soon turns north and crosses a col at 2506m between the Egesengrat and the main range. Steeply down from this into a vague, green, wet area, the Wilde Grube; through this and up on to the long, fine, high-level path, with great views beyond the Mutterberg Alm, and magnificently back towards the Schaufelspitze. Several rocky spurs must be negotiated, one quite steep, with fixed rope; one rather unstable. One has a tall 'stone man' and exceptionally fine views of the Wilde Pfaff, Zuckerhütl and Wilde Freiger. After the third spur the path climbs up to the Grawagrubennieder - a beautiful pass with a shapely rock tower; but the descent on the north side is very loose indeed and quite dangerous. There can be an awkward 'bad step' from loose rock to rotten ice when you reach the edge of the Hochmoos Glacier. Cross the glacier; then there is a further 3km of picturesque walking to the pleasingly situated Neue Regensburger Hut (2286m Cat. I).

In 1990 the Hochmoos Glacier had so far retreated that the "awkward bad step" had vanished, but coming up the valley from the Regensburger Hut, as we did on this occasion it was all too easy to stray off the path on to the glacier, which was not wholly free of crevasses.

Leaving the hut next morning you start on a traverse path, NE. After a kilometre of so fork left up a steep path. This rises to the west of the cliffs of the South spur of the Basslerjoch (2830m) with the col, the Schrimmennieder (2706m) always directly ahead. From the pass, an impressive view down to Ranalt over 1400m below. Beyond the pass the distance is greater than you might anticipate, for the path has to swing round in a huge arc before it drops to a level conclusion. During the latter part there are good views into the Oberbergtal.

The Franz-Senn Hut (2147m Cat. I), built in 1885 and enlarged in 1932 and 1962 is worthy of its dedication to Franz Senn, founder of the Alpenverein.   (1968)

From the Franz-Senn Hut to the Starkenberger Hut is the longest 'leg' of the 'round' (at least 6hrs: allow more), but also one of the most rewarding. Early in the day you have to weave in and out of gullies, with fixed ropes in places, and in one, even 'handles' fixed to the rock. There is also a mercifully short, very narrow track rising across extremely steep scree (but this is more intimidating in descent, when coming from the Starkenberger Hut). After this slow section you will reach the Sedugg Hochalm (2249m), *not* a ruin, despite the map, but friendly and hospitable. After this the Franz-Senn Way proves to be a fine path, traversing high above the Oberbergtal.

At the Seejöchl (2518m) above the See Alm with its beautiful lakes, the path swings round to the SE. It passes below the Schlicker Scharte (2456m) between the jagged Schlicker See Spitz (2804m; ascent not to be recommended) and the Burgstall Massif, and then traverses steep, loose scree. It feels very narrow and insecure and you may be glad when you turn a sharp corner and drop on firmer ground down to the hut.

The easiest descent from the Starkenberger Hut is the excellently engineered path to the Kreuzjoch, whence a two-stage chair-lift takes you painlessly down to Fulpmes. For purists and the impecunious there is a good path (115) to Neustift on the NE side of the Bachental. If doing the Stubai Round in reverse (ie. anti-clockwise) there is much to be said for starting on the chair-lift. (1990)

The Hoher Bergstall (2611m), the 'Hausberg' of the Starkenberger Hut, is easy (about 1hr), but very rewarding. Start as if for the Franz-Senn Hut, but soon go off to the right. The path is loose in places but the limestone scenery near the summit is exciting and the more distant views are magnificent. Not to be missed if you have time and energy. (1990)

2. THE SENNENJOCH (2289m) AND SCHLICKER ALM (1616m)

(Alternative name-forms: Sennesjoch, Sennesjöchl) This 'little' walk (involving, however, some 1340m (4400ft) of ascent - enough for a good day in Scotland) is typical of the many lower walks which can be extemporised from the valley.

Begin at Medraz and go up the slopes on the west side of the valley, past Gröbenhof to a 'Jausenstation' (refreshment house) called Vergör. Do not take the path to the right just before this or you will find yourself traversing towards Frohneben, the top station of the lowest chair-lift up from Fulpmes. If you *do* take this you must traverse back along a higher path to the Galtalm, more directly reached via Vergör. Food should be available here.

From the Galtalm take a good, almost level path for 2 or 3km to the Knappen Hut, another refreshment house, sometimes mistaken for the Starkenberger Hut.

Now take the path NNE from the Knappen Hut signposted for the Sennenjoch. Follow this, keeping left at a junction. (Right leads to the Grimmenkopf (2136m) a viewpoint at the end of the spur.) The upper part of Sennenjoch path is very fine, contouring above steep crags and eventually zig-zagging steeply up a spur. The Sennenjoch, when you reach it, is a barren enough spot but providing a sudden view of the great limestone cliffs and towers of the Kalkkögel. There is now a big top-station of the Sennjoch lift from the Schlicker Alm here, and a little to your right is the 'Panorama Restaurant' at the top of the Keuzjoch chair-lift. You cross the path from the Kreuzjoch to the Starkenberger Hut at this point. Continue down the NW side (it may be muddy) to the Zirmach Hut, a well-appointed alm, and from this on a jeep track to the Schlicker Alm (1616m). The Schlicker-Alm Wirtshaus is privately owned, 53 beds. There is also a charming church.

It is a road-trog now down to Frohneben. Then either: straight on down almost into Fulpmes until you find a pleasant path back to Medraz, or: take the traverse path almost due south until this joins your original ascent path; then down this via Gröbenhof to your starting-point.   (1968)

3. THE ELFER SPITZE (2505m)

Recommended for its scenery

Take the Elferlift from Neustift and walk up a good path to the Elfer Hut (2004m). Continue beyond the hut, ignoring the *Klettersteig* (protected rock-climb) to the Elfertürme, which goes off to the right. Far below you on the left is the Pinnistal and the rock-scenery around you can look truly Wagnerian, especially in moving mist. The final stage to the summit branches right and involves a rock-traverse and chimney-like fissure with (loose!) fixed ropes. Return to the main path but not to the hut. Instead, continue through the dramatically broken summit massif. The path takes you round the mountain high up on the Pinnistal side, to the Zwölfernieder (2335m), the pass from the Pinnistal to the Stubaital between the Elfer and the Zwölfer. If it is still there, an inscription on a boulder

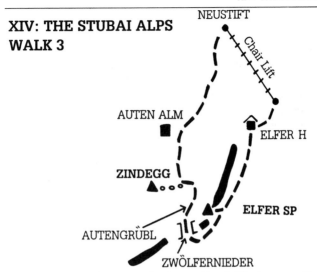

XIV: THE STUBAI ALPS
WALK 3

NEUSTIFT

Chair Lift

AUTEN ALM

ELFER H

ZINDEGG

ELFER SP

AUTENGRÜBL

ZWÖLFERNIEDER

points to a 'New Descent' to the Auten Alm (1658m), an excellently made zig-zag path down the Autengrübl. Below the 'Grübl' there is a fine natural alpine garden and a path to the left leading to Zindegg (2052m). Below the alm (refreshments) a good, old, path drops steeply through forestry, crossing the forestry road again and again (easy to miss) and eventually bringing you back to Neustift. (1990)

C. THE ÖTZTAL

(for description, see Ötztal Alps p111)
The Ötztal forms the western boundary of the Stubai Alps and the western approaches are made from it, as well as the entry to the valley series described in Section A. Thus the Gubener Hut (See Section A, Walk 3) can be reached from Umhausen up the Horlachtal, and the Winnebachsee Hut (See Section A, Walk 3) can be reached from Längenfeld via Gries in the Sulztal. If you do not branch left into the Winnebachtal you can continue unexcitingly up the Sulztal to the Amberger Hut (2135m. Cat. I). Two one-day walks are described here.

XIV: THE STUBAI ALPS
C. ÖTZTAL

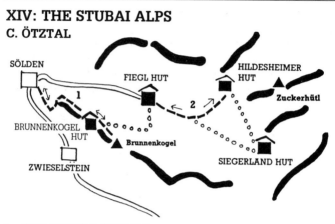

1. THE BRUNNENKOGEL (2775m)

The Brunnenkogel is the last top on the spur which divides the Windbachtal from the upper Ötztal and its branches the Gurglertal and Ventertal. Leave Sölden by Mühle (a ruined mill accounts for the name) and walk pleasantly SE through woods to the Stabl Alm and then due north to the Falkner Wirtshaus (1973m). The route is now more open, following the crest of the spur, with quite thrilling views of the Vent and Gurgl valleys. Finally, zig-zags bring you to the little Brunnenkogel Haus (2735m), with 2 beds and 16 mattress places, run by the Austrian Tourist Club (ÖTK), on the Vorderer Brunnenkogel. Refreshments here. It is then an easy ascent of 15mins to the big stone man on the Hinterer Brunnenkogel (2775m). (The ridge beyond, to the Rotkogel (2892m) is described as without difficulties, but beyond that the grading rises.) The summit of the Brunnenkogel is described by the German guidebook as having hardly any significance for the mountaineer: but it is a fine place to be, especially when a skittering of snow, and light through broken clouds, add distinction to the scene. Return the same way. (An alternative route up or down links the Brunnenkogel House and the Fiegl Hut (1959m privately run) in the Windachtal. There is a jeep from Sölden to the Fiegl Hut.)
(1966)

2. THE HILDESHEIMER HUT (2899m Cat. I)

This hut has a marvellous, if bleak, situation, looking out on the splendid Pfaffen Glacier backed by the snowy summit of the Zuckerhütl. It is approached from Sölden via the Windachtal. The path is quite steep at first and you are soon looking down on the 'toy' houses and church. You then find yourself on a good track in the high valley. This continues to the Fiegl Hut (1969m privately run). There is a jeep thus far which will save 2¹/₂hrs walking if you are short of time. Otherwise the path-walk is worth doing.

About 1¹/₂km beyond the Fiegl Hut there is a branch to the left (north). (The path straight on goes to the Siegerland Hut (2710m Cat. I), from which there is a high-level path to the Hildesheimer Hut.) Take this branch. It is the Aschenbrenner Way. It climbs steeply in zig-zags and soon you will have a fine view back down the Windachtal. At first the path - very well made - is among boulders and rough vegetation. Eventually you reach an open corner from which you see the hut (still 45mins away) above you and a little to your left. Further right the Pfaffen Glacier can be admired.

The hut stands above a tarn on high rock which falls away precipitously to the east, forming a magnificent 'dress circle' from which to view the Pfaffen Glacier and Zuckerhütl. More distant prospects to the SW include the Wildspitze group.

Except for the high level route to the Siegerland Hut already mentioned, all crossings and summit routes from this hut are glaciated and demanding, so for our one-day walk we simply return by the same route, enjoying the effects of afternoon light on the Windachtal.

The 'guidebook time' from the Fiegl Hut to the Hildesheimer Hut is 3hrs, but allow more unless you are very fit. When the writer visited the hut they wouldn't serve hot food in the afternoon after 2.30p.m., so be warned.   (1971)

XV: The Zillertal Alps
(AVE Group 35)

The Name: This group takes its name from the Zillertal, the next major valley to the east of the Wipptal (Brenner Pass), which leaves the main Inn Valley at Strass and runs in an almost straight line due south for some 27km to Mayrhofen, where it branches into four main tributary valleys (W to E): the Tuxer Tal, the Zemmgrund, the Stilluppgrund and the Zillergrund. But the mountain groups east and west of the Zillertal for two-thirds of its length, from Strass to Zell-am-Ziller, are the Kitzbühl Alps (Group 34) and the Tuxer Alps (Group 33) (formerly 'Tuxer Voralpen'), while the name Zillertal Alps is reserved primarily for the main E-W range that forms the Austro-Italian frontier, and about half their area is in Italy. Therefore, even if you do not intend to cross the frontier it is advisable to carry your passport when walking in this area. The walks described here are based on Mayrhofen, but for the sake of completeness the Alpenverein's 'official' boundaries are given.

Boundaries of the Group: (The group comprises: the Tuxer Hauptkamm, Zillertaler Hauptkamm, Pfunderer Berge and Gerlos Group.) Zell-am-Ziller - the Gerlostal - the Gerlos Pass - the R. Salzach to its junction with the Krimmler Ache - the Krimmler Tal to Birnlücke on the frontier - Prettau (St. Valentin or Predoi) - the Arhntal and the Taufener Tal to Bruneck (Brunico) - the R. Reinz to its junction with the Eisack (Isarco) - the R. Eisack (Isarco) to Brenner - the Wipptal to its junction with the Schmirnbach - up the Schmirn Tal and the Kasener Bach to the Tuxer Joch - down the Tuxer Tal to Mayrhofen - Zillertal to Zell-am-Ziller.

The area is approached from the Inn Valley and most visitors from Britain will aim first at Innsbruck. An interesting and less busy way, which leads direct to the Zillertal, is over the Achen Pass.

Mayrhofen is one of the best known and most visited summer resorts in Austria. There is plenty of accommodation and a campsite. It does strike one, however, as being 'a resort'. It has lost the character of a traditional Austrian village and at the same time

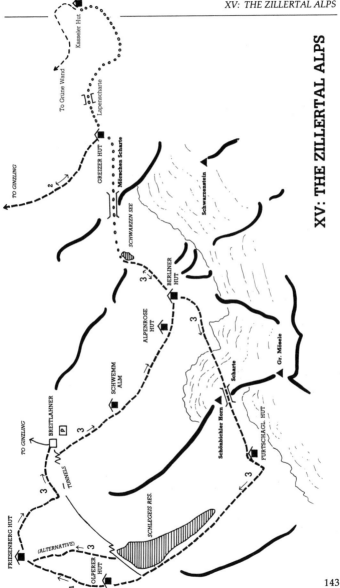

seems to have little if any independent industrial life. The writer also has reason to endorse Philip Tallantire's warning: 'Anyone who has the misfortune to coincide with a wet week in the Zillertal has my sympathy. The clouds drift aimlessly in circles, the mist rises out of the valleys and the rain descends'. (*Felix Austria* II Zillertal Alps pp.7 & 8.)

Sadly, all the Zillertal's tributary valleys have already been raped. The Tuxer Tal has been heavily developed for summer as well as winter skiing; the Zemmgrund has a fantastic toll road right up to the huge Schlegeis Reservoir, which was built in the 1960s, drowning a whole deep valley, houses and all; the Stillupp Tal, the approach valley to the Kasseler Hut (2177m Cat. I), also has its motor road and reservoir; even the Zillergrund, which in 1977 could still be believed to have been 'the loneliest of all the Mayrhofen valleys' - as it was described in the 1971 German guidebook - now has buses as far as Bärenbad and a reservoir above that; but no doubt the Plauener Hut (2363m Cat. I) remains as *gemütlich* as ever on its barren site below the glaciers of the Reichenspitze (3303m). Only the Floitengrund, which branches SE off the Zemmgrund at Ginzling, is still virtually unspoiled despite a mini-bus road as far as the Sulzen- Alpe, and its scenery is of the grandest and most romantic: the walk up it to the Greizer Hut (2226m Cat. I) is strongly to be recommended (Walk 2).

There are, of course, plenty of short walks from Mayrhofen, and their number can be increased by first getting out of the valley by cable-car.

The Penken Lift, for example takes you up to near the Penkenjochhaus (2095m), a vulgar place with loud canned music, whence you can without difficulty reach the Rastkogel (2762m).

There are also very beautiful valley walks such as that up the Sondergrund from 'In der Au' (toll road from Zillergrund), and many places of refreshment such as the Zimmereben and the Alpenrose (1398m). If you intend to wander in the forests, for instance on the eastern slopes of the main valley, be sure you have an up-to-date map, as it is perilously easy to get seriously lost. This is true even if you are using Walter Klier's *Bergwanderungen in den Zillertaler Alpen.*

The major summits of the Zillertal main range, such as the

Hochfeiler (3510m), the Grosse Mösele (3478m), Turnerkamp (3276m), Schwarzenstein (3368m), Grosse Löffler (3376m) etc., all involve glacier crossing and are quite serious mountains, even when technically not difficult. The range nevertheless has a 'plum' for more modest walkers in the form of the Schönbichler Horn (3133m), a three-thousander that lies virtually on a relatively easy hut-to-hut route.

The principal hut-to-hut walk on this side of the main range - which should present no serious difficulties to users of this guide - is: Mayrhofen - Stilluppgrund - Kasseler Hut (2177m) - Lapen-Scharte (2700m) - Greizer Hut (2226m) - Mörchenscharte (2870m) - Berliner Hut (2040m) - Schönbichler Scharte and Horn (3133m) - Furtschagl Hut (2295m) - Schlegeisgrund - then bus to Mayrhofen. (But as the writer has not walked it all, only part of it is fully described here.)

The approaches to the Kasseler and Greizer Huts are given here (Walks 1 & 2) and these huts can be linked to the Berliner Hut in order to complete the Zillertal High Level Way.

1. KASSELER HUT (2178m)

Except for experienced rock-climbers this hut is at present the start of the east-west traverse of the Zillertal High Level Route, part of the Central Alpine Way (502).

Catch a mini-bus up the Stilluppgrund to "Grüne Wand" (1436m), or failing that, a bus to the Wasserfall Hotel by the Stilluppspeicher - which adds up to 2hrs road-walking.

A little above the "Grüne Wand" is the bottom station of the goods-cable to the hut. If you are lucky you may be able to send your rucksack up on this. (We could not do so, as it was too windy to send the box down.) The beautiful path (519) (the Aschaffenburg High Level Route) zig-zags up a steep valley past many waterfalls towards a fine cirque at the base of which you cross a waterfall on a fairly dramatic bridge and zig-zag up the cirque to the right until you reach the hut. If not aiming at the Greizer Hut, return the same way.

(The route to the Greizer Hut over the Lapenscharte (2701m) is unglaciated but not to be underestimated. It may well take you more than the official 4-5hrs.)

2. THE FLOITENGRUND AND THE GREIZER HUT (2226m Cat. I)

Of the valley walks radiating to the south of Mayrhofen that up the unspoiled Floitengrund to the Greizer Hut merits full description.

Drive or catch the bus to Ginzling. From Ginzling you may drive as far as the Tristenbachalm (car park) or catch a mini-bus (if you are lucky) to the Sulzenalpe. The walk above here is probably the most romantic valley walk in the area. It is a narrow valley, green and partially wooded at first. Higher it has more scattered boulders. Higher still you feel the weight of the steep mountain slopes impending on each side; the path is forced near the stream and the glacier and permanent snow at the valley head can be seen. When the hut comes into view it is higher and rather to the left. The path becomes steeper, the valley stonier and as we climb to the left, the stream is below us on our right. Now, over stony slopes the path climbs the valley side in zig-zags until the hut is reached, perched on a sort of spur, looking out on the ice-fall of the Floiten Glacier, and also away down the valley.

(This cosy hut lies on the main hut-to-hut route between the Kasseler Hut (4-5hrs over the Lapenscharte (2700m)) and the Berliner Hut (5hrs over the Mörchenscharte (2870m).) Both routes are glacier-free, well made, well marked and highly praised in the German guidebook.)

If not hut-to-hutting, return same way down the Floitengrund.

3. THE BERLINER HUT (2040m Cat. I) TO THE FRIESENBERG HAUS (2498m Cat. I) (via the Schönbichler Horn (3133m) Furtschagl Haus (2295m Cat. I) and the Olperer Hut (2389m Cat. I)).

This walk of about 4 days is in effect the latter part of the major hut-to-hut walk on the north side of the main range, with a supplement.

Drive or take the bus to Breitlahner (1257m) at the junction of the Zamsergrund and the Zemmgrund. (You can pay in advance for so many days' parking.) Walk SE up the Zemmgrund to the Grawandhaus (1640m privately owned). This gets you away from the toll road, but there is a bulldozed road thus far. The house is pleasantly situated with a good view down the valley. Refreshments available. On a fine day you will not be alone! There is no traffic above the Grawandhaus but a heavily worn path through alpine meadows with scattered trees as far as the Alpenrose-Wirtshaus

(1875m privately owned), a popular goal for valley walkers. Above the Alpenrose there are fewer folk and the scenery becomes more mountainous. The Berliner Hut (2040m Cat. I) is very large, like a hotel. The 'Gaststube' suggests a baronial hall - and the food is worthy of one. Even so, you may find yourself sleeping in a very humble *Nebenhaus* (annexe) with the sound of the mountain stream to lull you to sleep. The scenery is as good as the food, too.

If you are early enough in the day it is more than worthwhile to walk up to the Schwarzen See (2469m) on the way to the Mörchen Scharte and the Greizer Hut. It is a walk with magnificent views: to the SW the Gr. Mösele and its associated glaciers, by now probably catching the lower light of the afternoon, and to the SE the Schwarzenstein and its glacier. The lake is a true mountain tarn, reflecting steep crags and grassy slopes. (About 1¹/₂hrs up.)

Next morning it is well to get away before 6.30a.m. The path (502) leaves the hut almost due south but swings round in a big curve towards SW. You lose a good deal of height to begin with, crossing several streams. Then the path turns almost due south and later climbs steeply in zig-zags towards W and SW, at first on open ground and later more interestingly and rockily up the ridge called the Krähenfuss (the Crowbar), with at least one fixed rope, which may be broken. The views to the south of the Waxeck (Waxegg) Glacier and the black ridge of the Rossrugg leading up to the Rossruggspitze (3304m) are most impressive. The interest of the upper sections depends upon snow conditions: you may have quite a lot, and an ice-axe is an advantage. Before the final pyramid of the Schönbichler Horn there is a glorious section of snow-ridge,like walking the ridge of a house, with the Schönbichler Glacier on one side and the Waxeck Glacier on the other. The final stages are scrambly with fixed ropes. The Pass (3081m) is a mere 150ft or so from the Schönbichler Horn summit (3133m), which is reached without difficulty. The situation is more rewarding than that on many a higher top. To the NW a sharp rock ridge leads to the Grosse Greiner, a mere 66m higher, while SSE the same ridge carries the eye right away along and up to the snow-summit of the Gr. Mösele (3478m). To the east you can see back to the Berliner Hut and beyond, while to the WSW, far below, you can already see your day's goal, the Furtschaglhaus, backed by the vast, black precipices of the Hochsteller (3097m). But the descent is far easier than the ascent via the Krähenfuss.

The Furtschaglhaus is also run by the Berlin Section of the Alpenverein, but you may find its atmosphere quite different: it depends on the wardens. (NB. Many people 'do' the Schönbichler Horn as an end in itself from this easier side.)

The route you have just followed between the two huts is, not surprisingly, called the Berliner Way. (Allow a good 6hrs.)

From the Furtschaglhaus the path drops steeply in zig-zags near waterfalls into the valley now inundated by the Schlegeis Reservoir, which admittedly has its own beauty for those of us who did not know the valley before. The track follows the western side of this to the Schlegeis Kiosk, the end of the toll road and bus route. A little beyond the inlet formed by the Zamser Bach, route 502 leaves the road and climbs steeply to the Olperer Hut (2389m Cat. I), another hut of the Berlin Section. Superb view of the Schlegeis Reservoir backed by the mountains and glaciers of the main Zillertal chain. You may well be early enough in the day to continue on the Berliner Way (now 526) to the Friesenberg Haus (2498m. Cat. I) only 2hrs or so away. This is a rewarding and easy, high-level route with a small sting in its tail. You have to drop quite a way to the Friesenberg See (2444m), a desolate tarn, and then climb about 50m up to the hut.

There is also a direct path to the Friesenberg Haus from the Dominikus Hut (1810m privately owned) by the dam. This is a pleasant route, but offering less extensive views than the high-level path. (The original Dominikus Hut was drowned in the reservoir.)

The descent next day to Breitlahner is most enjoyable, but do not underestimate it: it involves 1250m of descent, just over 4000ft. You leave the hut on Path 530 ENE and E, actually climbing a few feet at the start and then following a high-level path not unlike the previous day's. Eventually the path swings towards SE and drops steeply through increasing forest. It touches the toll road just above the upper entrance to the series of tunnels above Breitlahner but leaves it immediately to run parallel with the Zamser Bach down to Breitlahner, where you catch a bus or recover your car.   (1977)

4. AHORNSPITZE (2976m)

The 'Hausberg' of Mayrhofen

Catch the Ahorn cable-car. (Remember that the last trip down is at 5p.m.) Walk on Path 514 to the Edel Hut (2238m), enjoying the views. From the Edel Hut a rising path takes you to the foot of the summit pyramid, a long scramble (perhaps as much as 500m) with red waymarks, not always clear. The route includes a rock traverse with fixed rope, a pleasant rocky rib and a loose gully leading to a tiny saddle between two summits, of which the north, with cross, is the higher, though the south one is impressive. Return the same way.   (1993)

(It is also possible to go down to Mayrhofen via the Alpenrose on Path 42.)

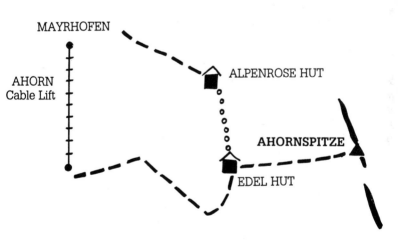

XV: ZILLERTAL ALPS WALK 4

XVI: The Venediger Group
(AVE Group 36)

Boundaries of the Group: The most recent definition of this group, which differs somewhat from earlier definitions, is: Krimml - the Salzach as far as Mittersill - the Felber Bach to the Felber Tauern (St. Pöltener Hut) - the Tauernbach to Matrei-in-Osttirol - R. Isel to Huben - the Schwarzach to the Jagdhausalm - the Klammljoch - the Klammlbach to Sand-in-Taufers - the Ahrntal to Prettau - the Birnlücke - the Krimmler Achental to Krimml.

In effect this is the next principal mountain group east of the Zillertal Alps. It has distinct northern and southern approaches, linked since 1967 by the Felber Tauern Strasse from Mittersill, up the Felber Tal and the Amertal, through the long Felber Tauern Tunnel (toll) and down the Tauern Tal to Matrei and beyond.

The base for all the walks described here (and those in the next group, the Granatspitz Group) is Matrei-in-Osttirol. This charming little town, still not unpleasantly overdeveloped, lies at the junction of the Tauerntal and the Virgental. It has plenty of accommodation, a good, though not cheap campsite, a variety of eating places and good bus services. The area, particularly the Virgental, has been greatly, but not objectionably developed in recent years from the walker's viewpoint, with new paths and new huts - even with high-level 'Nature Trails' intended to appeal to the age group kindly designated 'Senioren' by the Alpenverein, a word that seems to imply much less decrepitude than 'OAP'. Around Matrei there are also plenty of half day strolls and longer low-level walks.

The major hut-to-hut route is the Venediger-Hohenweg, which links eight high huts in a great arc from the St. Pöltener Hut in the east to the Clara Hut in the south of the group. It is an outstanding route, some sections of which require mountaineering experience and involve scrambling, exposure and glacier crossings. Part of it is described here (Walk 2).

The Grosser Venediger (Walk 1) itself is one of the easiest of the highest mountains of the eastern alps. The easiest ascents are from

XVI: THE VENEDIGER GROUP

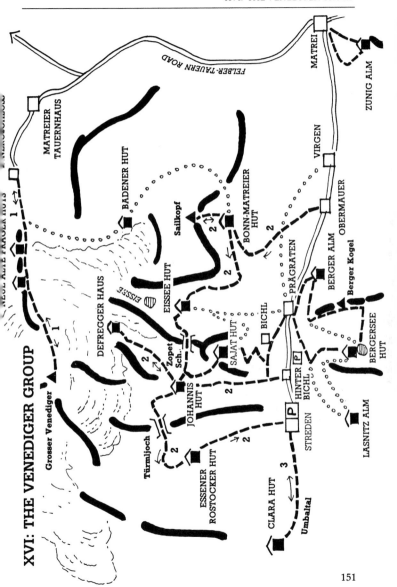

the Defregger Haus and the Neue Prager Hut. The former is shorter; the latter is described here.

1.   THE NEUE PRAGER HUT (2796m Cat. I) AND THE GROSSER VENEDIGER (3674m)

From Matrei drive or take the bus up the Tauerntal to the famous and anciently sited Matreier Tauernhaus. From here there is a road up to Innergschloss: you may drive up this before 9.00a.m., otherwise a mini-bus is available: or walk! If you walk you can linger *en route* by the Felsen Kapelle (Rock Chapel), once free-standing but destroyed by rockfall, so now built 'in' the rock. Excellent views of the Grosser Venediger along here. Soon after this we reach Innergschloss (1725m) a real alm village with a useful Wirtshaus.

(In 1978 the Alpenverein established from here the Gletscherweg (Glacier-way) Innergschloss, a 4hr walk which follows an old shepherd's path to a fine viewpoint for observing the Schlatten Kees, the glacier descending from the Grosser Venediger on this side. For the return route the round walk uses the main path from the Neue Prager Hut.)

Beyond Innergschloss, just where the path steepens, there is the start of a good cableway which, if you can cope with its primitive field telephone, will take your rucksacks up the next steep section, over 700m of ascent in just over $1^{1}/_{2}$km. It is an act of faith to leave your bags there. To recover them at the top station, near the Alte Prager Hut (2489m Cat. I) you must make a slight diversion. This hut, first built in 1872, was restored and put into use again in 1972 after having been destroyed in an avalanche. Catering here is limited and it is best to proceed to the Neue Prager Hut, 300m higher at 2796m and still 1km away, 1km that takes 1hr, making 5hrs 'guidebook time' if you walk all the way from the Matreier Tauernhaus. It is an extremely popular hut but the warden has many mattresses to supplement the 43 beds and 42 Lager when the hut is full.

(From this hut the Venediger-Hohenweg goes NE to the St. Pöltener Hut - a hard 6hrs - and S to the Badener Hut, said to be the finest section of the whole Hohenweg.)

Relatively easy for its altitude though the Grosser Venediger is, its ascent involves a crevassed glacier, so only a roped party with ice-axes and appropriate experience should attempt it: failing these, pay for a guide.

A good time to set out is 5.00a.m. The track starts by leading down to the edge of the glacier, the Schlatten Kees. Then the beaten track climbs to the left of, and parallel with the Niederer Zaun, a rock-rib almost 1km long, up to point 2993m, the so-called 'roping-up point' (Anseilplatz), and rightly so-called, for almost immediately after it we encounter a crevassed section. While roping up you will probably want to snap the eastern view of dawn and the Gross Glockner. The crevassed section passed, the rest is sheer slog up the glacier to its less steep upper section, the Oberer Keesboden at about 3300m, and finally up the steeper final section to the summit at 3674m, with magnificent views, especially to the south and to the east, where the spire of the Gross Glockner dominates the scene beyond the Grosser Muntanitz.

Return to the hut by the same route, remembering that snow bridges may by now be less secure.　　　(1967 + information 1984)

2. A SECTION OF THE VENEDIGER-HOHENWEG

(4 days without the Sailkopf) Obermauern - Bonn-Matreier Hut (2750m Cat. I) - Eissee Hut (2500m privately owned) - Zopet Scharte (2958m) - Johannis Hut (2121m. Cat. I) - Türmljoch (2790m) - Essener Rostocker Hut (2208m Cat. I) - Streden.

This is the heart of the southern section of the Venediger Hohenweg, except that the strict Hohenweg goes from the Eissee Hut direct to the Defregger Haus and then to the Johannis Hut. In addition to the basic walk, descriptions are included for climbing the Sailkopf (3209m) and visiting the Defregger Haus (2962m Austrian Tourist Club, ÖTK). Other possibilities are also mentioned.

There is a good bus service up the Virgental from Matrei and reasonable parking in most of the villages. The last free parking is at Hinterbichl, and at the road end at Streden there is a very large paying car park. If doing the walk here described it is better to use the bus.

The shortest and steepest route to the Bonn-Matreier Hut begins at Obermauern, whose church is worth a visit. Its interior is nearly covered with 'comic strip' murals. primarily illustrating the life of Christ. Follow the hut signpost NW out of Obermauern on a motor road at first and then up very steep meadows on a big spur picturesquely called Eselsrücken, the Donkey's Back. At the top of the steep section there is a welcome refreshment house, the Niljochhütte, rather to the left of the path. Longer, less painfully steep paths from Prägraten to the west and Virgen to the east join our route here. Fine views up and down the Virgental.

The path continues, less steeply, up the Nilltal, a big grassy cwm that gathers all the heat the sun pours into it. The path keeps to the left of the stream. Towards the head of the valley you will find the valley station of the hut's goods cableway. In 1967 it was possible to send your rucksacks up on this. The hut warden, who was also a shepherd, used to ride up on it, quite illegally, no doubt, at the end of his day's work. Nowadays, thanks to helicopter deliveries, the cableway has a disused air about it, and the present hut warden (the shepherd's son) most certainly does not ride up in the box!

Above this the path climbs steeply and traverses the head of the valley in a huge arc from west to east below a desolate area called the Sandboden, followed by a final pull up to the hut, which stands on a prominent spur at 2750m. Near the hut is a little rock-chapel. Built in 1932 and in recent years enlarged with great skill and taste, the hut is unique in that it is run jointly by an Austrian Alpine Club Section (Matrei) and a German (Bonn), the joint enterprise having been set up at a time when no one would have dreamed that Bonn would become the capital of the western half of a divided Germany and later of a re-united Germany.

From this hut you can climb the Sailkopf (3209m), one of the easiest and nearest summits (about 2hrs ascent). The route is due north up a big, steepish cwm between the Sailspitze (3137m) to the west and Rauhkopf (3070m) - also easy from the hut - to the east. The ascent may be up loose scree, or you may be lucky and have 300m of cramponing on frozen snow. (It was thus in 1967.) Aim at a rough and ridgy col to the east of the Sailkopf, then scramble on loose rock to the summit. There is a wonderful view of the Gross Glockner and a rock shaped like a giant eagle to fill the foreground of your photograph. To the south lie the hut and the depths of the Virgental. Return same way.

(The path east from the Bonn-Matreier Hut over the Galtenscharte (2892m) is 'for experienced mountaineers only' and the signpost advises asking the hut warden about conditions. The far side of the Galtenscharte has, as a

Dutch climber who had just come over it, said, 'no proper rock'. The route is exposed and the fixed ropes in bad condition (1984). It is much harder in descent i.e. *to* the Badener Hut - than in ascent.)

Our present walk takes us west to the comparatively new Eissee Hut (2500m privately owned) at the head of the Timmeltal. This is a very fine section of the Venediger Hohenweg, at first traversing high above the Virgental and then running almost due north up the eastern side of the Timmeltal. Although privately owned, the hut has all the best qualities of an Alpenverein Hut - including 'Teewasser'.

The route from here to the Johannis Hut begins to the west, but soon turns north into the high valley at the head of which lies the Eissee from which the hut takes its name - a. pleasant afternoon's walk.

(The continuation of the path beyond the Eissee leads to the Wallhorntörl (3045m), after which a glacier crossing leads to the Defregger Haus - the strict Hohenweg route.)

A little way up the valley the path to the Johannis Hut forks left (sign) across the stream, and traverses upwards. Magnificent views across the valley to the Eichham (3371m) and the Hexenkopf (3313m). The path does not lead, as it appears to, to the snow-slope below the col but, near a sign warning about stonefall (Steinschlag) bears right and continues on a well waymarked route (but follow it carefully!) up friable rock protected by fixed ropes in places. The stonefall danger is from parties higher up on the loose rock: it is good to be the first party of the day.

The Zopetscharte (2958m) is a grand place to be, with splendid views east and west and the Zopetspitze rising sharply to the north. The descent on the west to the Johannis Hut presents no difficulties. It runs almost due west down a big stony corrie, eventually swinging north on the 'Zopet' pastures to get below a big spur. About here note the path to the Sajat Hut. There is a rough, steep section of path immediately above the Johannis Hut.

In this area you will see little numbered signs. These rather comically relate to the 'Nature Trails' that have been established up here: for whom?

At the Johannis Hut (2121m Cat. I) we are, in the words of Philip Tallantire, 'treading hallowed ground', for this is one of the oldest huts (1857) purpose-built for mountaineers on the southern side of the eastern alps. It retains much of its *Gemütlichkeit* and in 1984 had a staff of charming girls and a friendly dog called Bello.

From here the Defregger Haus (2962m Austrian Tourist Club, ÖTK) is easy to reach and worth visiting even if you do not intend to climb the Grosser Venediger from it. It is the highest hut in the Venediger Group and offers the shortest route to the Venediger summit. The path to the hut from the Johannis Hut runs up a vast rib between glaciers, and for once it is probably true to say, 'You can't miss it!'. A non-glaciated route from the huts to the east, by-passing the Johannis Hut and eventually joining this path, is under construction. (1984)

The direct route from the Virgental to the Johannis Hut starts at Hinterbichl (free parking and bus terminus). The old and picturesque path now survives only in sections as a dirt road has been made up the valley, first to a quarry and then more steeply and hairily to within a few yards of the hut. This road is closed to public traffic, but many climbers, hazarding insurance and the law, do drive their cars up it. My advice: don't! - but do accept a lift from a 'local' if offered.

The next 'leg' of the walk starts from the Johannis Hut for a few yards as if for the Defregger Haus, crossing a stream on a little bridge; but then you keep left and cross the Dorfer Bach by a natural bridge where it flows and falls dramatically through a gorge. Lasörling (accent on the second syllable) and her sister peaks to the south will probably be bathed in morning sunshine while you are still in cool, blue morning shadow.

The path goes up the valley, traversing below a rocky line of cliff called the Aderkamm. Turn the north end of this and proceed comfortably SW and W to the Türmljoch (2790m) - about $2^{1/2}$hrs. It is a beautiful spot, and the 'Little Tower' which gives it its name is a massive and shapely rock tower rearing up dramatically to 2845m on the southern side of the joch. The views E and NE are dominated by glacier scenery - the Rainer Kees. To the west the major feature on the far side of the Maurer Tal is the surprisingly named Malham Spitze (3378m), to the north of which the Reggentörl (3056m) gives the glacier route to the site of the former Essener Hut and thence to the Clara Hut (see Walk 3). Hamish Brown maintains that passes are as satisfying as peaks, and more logical. The Zopetscharte and

Türmljoch

Türmljoch tend to confirm his opinion.

The descent on the west, the Schweriner Way, begins with steep zig-zags, then runs almost due west, finally turning south by the Maurer Bach, towards the hut.

(To the north the glaciated route to the Warnsdorfer Hut over the Maurer Törl (3108m).)

The twin huts are finely placed and the sections concerned regret that at present there is no direct, high-level, unglaciated route to the Clara Hut. The glaciated route over the Reggen Törl leads to the *site* of the Neue Essener Hut, destroyed by an avalanche in 1958. (The Alte - Old - Essener Hut in the Passeiertal in S Tirol was lost to Italy in 1919). It is a full 2hrs beyond the site of the avalanched hut to the Clara Hut. The Rostocker Hut (built 1912) is an attractive stone building. The Essener Hut now attached to it was built 1962-4 and is a modern type of building, clad in grey.

The walk down the Maurer Tal is very beautiful, with fine waterfalls and gradually enriching greenery. As you get down towards Streden (Ströden) look out for the lovely little path by the Maurer Bach leading directly to the large Streden car park. The road back to the bus terminus at Hinterbichl is fairly dreary: try to beg or thumb a lift.

3.   THE CLARA HUT (2038m Cat. I)

This one-storey hut - built in 1872 and enlarged between 1969 and 1974 - is now rather isolated, the routes to other huts being long, and some glaciated. It is usually buried under the snow during the winter.

If you can get on wheels as far as Streden you will save a dull hour from the bus terminus at Hinterbichl. From Streden the path follows the upper valley of the R. Isel, the Umbal Tal, past the Pebell Alm (1513m) and the Ochser Hut (1933m). The valley is extremely beautiful and the stream has a celebrated series of cascades and falls, now threatened - of course! - by some philistine hydro-electric scheme or other. Ahead is the Rotspitze (3495m) and its associated peaks. Until - or unless - its stream is destroyed, this is one of the loveliest of 'hut trogs'.   (1967)

4.   THE SAJAT HUT (2600m), SAJATSCHARTE (2800m), THE SAJATHÖHENWEG AND THE JOHANNIS HUT (2121m)

The Sajat Hut was opened in 1974 having been built by members of the Kratzer family who had farmed these high meadows for generations. It is a curiously beautiful building variously described by its creators as a snail-shell and as a castle in the mountains. It can be approached from Prägraten and is linked by high-level paths with the Eissee Hut and the Johannis Hut.

If on the bus, get off at Prägraten, but if you have a car save yourself nearly 200m of uninteresting start, chiefly on tarmac, by driving up to the signposted car park between Bichl and Frössach. The path begins up the edge of woods, ENE, but soon turns west.

(At a parting of the ways the right-hand route leads roughly east across the meadow-slopes into the Timmel Tal, where there is a further choice of approaching the Sajat Hut via the Prägratener Höhenweg, of continuing straight up the valley to the Eissee Hut, or of climbing steeply up the east side of the valley to join the Venediger Höhenweg on its way to the Bonn Matreier Hut.)

Our route, known as the Katinweg, continues NW through the woods, then crosses a stream, traverses west across meadows radiant with flowers and grasses, then NE and past the cave formerly used by the farmers as their sleeping-place when out working on the meadows. A little higher and the hut comes into view on the grassy lip of the great corrie in which it lies surrounded on three sides by a horseshoe of rocky ridges and summits. Many zig-zags lead quite easily now to the hut.

There is a warm welcome here in every sense. The hut has a fine open wood stove, and as you are public-spirited you will no doubt have responded to the notice down in the woods asking you to carry up a log. The owners also work in close conjunction with the Austrian Alpine Club and you will be given concessions here, if a member, just as if it were one of the Club's own huts.

(From here the hut builders have provided two protected scrambles on to the Kreuzspitze (3164m) and the Roten Säule (2879m), the latter being the easier. Or you can simply return to the valley by following the path into the Timmel Tal.)

However, it is a pleasant hut in which to spend the evening and night before following the Sajat Höhenweg to the Johannis Hut next morning.

Amusingly, the Kratzers have designated their three high-level routes as Nature Trails(!) and you will find from time to time little wooden signs with numbers. Guides (i.e. leaflets) to the trails are said to be available.

From the hut, following the markings with care in order to avoid sheer 'grot', go NW to the obvious nick in the ridge, the Sajatscharte (2750m). The way is steep and unstable towards the top. On the far side a finely engineered path sometimes actually blasted out of the rock, traverses the steep sides of the Tanzboden (2879m) and the Knappen Spitze until it reaches the high pastures below the Zopetscharte. Here, after a while, it joins the path from the Eissee Hut over the Zopetscharte, and so to the Johannis Hut as described in Walk 2.

Go down the Dorfer Tal from this hut, using as much as you can of the old path and keeping off the road wherever possible. Just beyond a crucifix called the Wiesenkreuz you will find a rising path to the left which leads you directly back to the car park at Bichl.

(1985)

5. THE BERGERSEE HUT (2182m), THE BERGER KOGEL (2656m) AND THE BERGER ALM.

This walk and the following one are in the Lasörling Group (stress on the second syllable) on the south side of the Virgental.

Get off the bus at the west end of Prägraten and walk down a signposted road, over the Isel, to a sawmill. (If you have a car, park at the sawmill.)

Follow the forest road until a steep path on the left is signposted to the Berger See and Hut.

(An alternative is to continue on the forest road to the Lasnitz Alm, whence the Bergersee Hut can be reached by means of a good high-level path which traverses round the north end of Muhs (2666m). Many walkers take this route to link the huts.)

The direct route to the Bergersee Hut climbs steeply until it is high above the Zopatnitzenbach in its gorge-like valley. The extremely picturesque path now runs fairly level until the stream is crossed. It then climbs to the splendid waterfall issuing from the lake - a waterfall that provides the hut with its private electricity. (About $2^1/_2$-3hrs)

The hut lies pleasantly by the lake and gets hundreds of day-visitors. There is a crude raft on which children play, and you can quickly walk round the lake. The actual walking is damp and dull, but the viewpoints reached are photogenic.

Few people spend the night here, though the accommodation and facilities are excellent. We had the hut to ourselves. The owners say it is not well placed to encourage overnighting. There are no concessions for AAC members, but you can get the usual 'Teewasser'.

From the hut follow the path east up to the Bergertörl (2500m), whence, if you continued down the other side you would reach Bobojach or Obermauern. Instead, turn left and follow the broad south ridge to the summit of the Berger Kogel (2656m), really an outlier of the Lasörling (3098m) and in itself a magnificent viewpoint.

Descend by the north ridge, which is much rockier and steeper than the south ridge, especially at the top. When you get on to the rather muddy pastures below be careful not to miss the way, as the waymarking is unsatisfactory. It is important to keep NW past a new alm hut to the Wetterkreuz (2153m.) Here you join the much more used and better waymarked direct path from the Bergersee

Wilde Freiger and the Grunau See, Stubai Tal.
Speicher Schlegeis, Zillertal

Sudetendeutsch Hut, Granatspitz
Tischkogel, Goldberg Group

Hut to the Berger Alm. Turn right and follow this pleasantly through bits of open woodland and pastures to the alm, where refreshments and friendliness are to be found.

To complete the round to Prägraten, and return to your car, if it is at the sawmill, follow the Prägraten sign at the alm. The path through the woods down into the valley is very steep. When you reach the valley floor, turn left and follow a good track back to the sawmill.

(If you have no car at Prägraten you can descend from the alm directly to Bobojach and catch a bus there.) (1985)

6. ZUNIG ALM (1846m)

This modest walk in the Lasörling Group starts in Matrei and could be regarded by the more ambitious walker as merely the first leg of the strenuous 6hr ascent of Zunig (2771m) which dominates the town on the south-west.

It is also confusing, not always well signed, and road developments have already put the German guidebook out-of-date.

If you are starting from the campsite aim at Bichl (NOT the Bichl up the valley near Prägraten) and then for Guggenberg. There is parking at this little hamlet, and indeed, many people drive this far - perhaps a good idea! From here signposted forest tracks and paths (if you can spot them) lead eventually to the alm, where food is available. It is in an open situation, with a glimpse of the Grossglockner.

(Apart from the ascent of Zunig - a further 3hrs at least - there is a lake to visit, some $^3/4$hr above the alm, or a round walk to be done via the Arnitz Alm.)

The old forest paths are easier to follow in descent, and you will find a 'short cut' to Matrei signposted. This is a good way to go down even if you ultimately lose it and have to finish on the road.

(1985)

XVII: The Villgratner Berge
(AVE Group 38)

Boundaries of the Group: Staller Sattel - Staller Almbach - Schwarzbach to junction with Isel - Isel to Lienz - Drautal - Toblach - Rienz to Olach -Antholzer Tal - Staller Sattel.

This group, lying partly in Italy at its western end and evidently taking its name from the Villgratner Bach, which penetrates it deeply from the south, has many paths but only one Alpenverein Hut, the Hochsteinhütte, though it also has two privately run huts, both well placed in relation to some of the group's highest summits and both easily accessible on drivable roads.

The best base for the one walk described here is Lienz, for details of which see Group XX (AVE Group 41).

THE BÖSES WEIBELE (STRICKKOFL: 2521m) FROM THE HOCHSTEIN HUT (2023m)

This class III hut, built in 1895 and rebuilt in 1920, is only about 10mins walk above the car park at the top of the road from Leisach (toll), but don't go to the hut yet. Instead, follow a path, level at first, signed for the Böses Weibele. At a fork, don't go straight on to the Gamperl Ski-hut, but take the right-hand path, which soon joins the main ridge-path - wide and rather stony. To the N and NW you have a good view already of the Schober Group across the Isel valley. At the next fork keep left: the right fork goes down to the Isel.

The route is easy and even picturesque in places. From the summit of the Böses Weibele (the Wicked Little Woman) you can see the snow-covered Venediger and Glockner groups, and the Hochschober, highest summit of the Schober Group. You can also see all the way back to the Hochstein and its hut. To the south are the Lienz Dolomites and to the east is Lienz. Sharply rising behind the Hochstein is the Rauchkofel. Below it, to its left you can see the Tristacher See.

On the way back aim straight for the Hochsteiner Hut: don't drop down to the right of the ridge near the Gamperl Ski-hut.

Anywhere on the way you may encounter a herd of beautiful and friendly horses, chiefly Haflingers. It is easy going now to the Hochstein (2057m) with a large war memorial cross, and somewhat further, the Hochstein Hut (2023m). From here you can see not only the whole of Lienz, the Tristacher See (with campsite) and the Rauchkofel, but even the Karlsbader Hut in the Lienz Dolomites (see XXV). In a very few minutes you are back to the car park.

(1995)

(The Hochstein Hut can, of course be reached on foot or partly by chair-lift (when it is running).

Beyond the Böses Weibele the ridge *does* continue to the Rotsteinberg (2696m), but the route is *much more difficult*. Only attempt this if you are sure of your skill and experience - and allow at least 5hrs for getting back to the Böses Weibele, and another 1-1¹/₂hrs to the Hochstein Hut.)

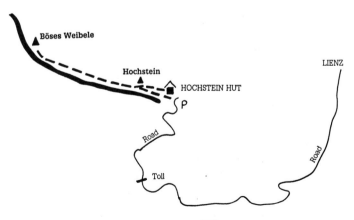

XVII: VILLGRATNER BERGE

XVIII: The Granatspitz Group
(AVE Group 39)

The Name: The mountain that gives its name to the group, the Granatspitze (3085m, accent on the second syllable) is by no means the highest, in fact it is the 9th in height. Note that *Granat* means 'garnet'. These are *NOT* granite mountains (German: *Granit)* but consist of gneiss, hornblende and even serpentine. An alternative name is the Landeck Group.

Boundaries of the Group: This is a long (north to south) narrow group, lying between and linking the Venediger Group and the Glockner Group. The R. Salzach from Mittersill to Uttendork - The Stubachtal - Einziger Boden - Grünsee - the Weissenbach to the Weiss See - Kalser Tauern - Dorfer See - Dorfer Tal - Kals - the Kalserbach to its junction with the Isel - the Isel to Matrei - the Tauernbach - Felber Tauern - Felbertal - Mittersill.

The walks described are based on Matrei (see *Venediger Group).*

1. THE SUDETENDEUTSCH HOHENWEG AND THE GROSSER MUNTANITZ.

Kals-Matreier Törl Haus (2207m privately owned) - Sudetendeutsch Hut (2650m Cat. I) - Kleiner Muntanitz (3192m) - Grosser Muntanitz (3232m).

Even in the late 1960s the trog up to the Kals-Matreier Törl Haus on a jeep track was pretty dull. Today it is doubtful whether anyone bothers with this $3^{1}/_{2}$hr walk, for one of the major developments in Matrei has been the Goldried Bergbahn, a chair-lift in two stages from the village to the saddle between Matrei and Kals. From the top station is the so-called Europa Panoramaweg, a 2hr walk to the top-station of a similar lift, the Bergbahn Glocknerblick, that comes up from Kals. This tourist walk has the distinction that from it no fewer than 63 three-thousand metre mountains can be seen. As it is only 1hour's walk from the lift to the Kals-Matreier Törl Haus most walkers will probably choose to save a day, spend their money and use the lift.

If you want a diversion, take a path south from the Panoramaweg

XVIII: THE GRANAT-SPITZ GROUP

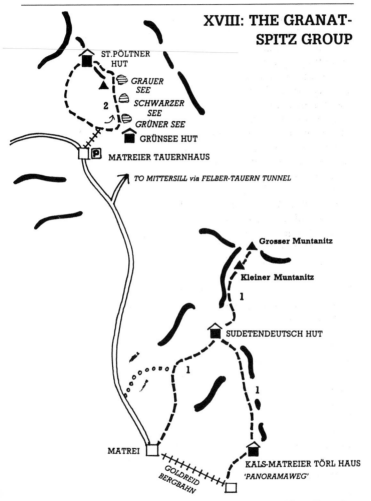

ST.PÖLTNER HUT

GRAUER SEE

2

SCHWARZER SEE

GRÜNER SEE

GRÜNSEE HUT

MATREIER TAUERNHAUS

TO MITTERSILL via FELBER-TAUERN TUNNEL

Grosser Muntanitz

Kleiner Muntanitz

1

SUDETENDEUTSCH HUT

1

1

MATREI

KALS-MATREIER TÖRL HAUS

GOLDREID BERGBAHN

'PANORAMAWEG'

(or from the Törl Haus, if you have walked to it) and walk to the Roten Kogel (2762m) - strongly reminiscent of Torridon, and chiefly of the Am Fasarinan pinnacles on Liathach.

If you do stay the night at the Törl Haus you will probably find

165

it quiet after the last lifts have gone down.

The Sudetendeutsch Hohenweg starts due north from the Kals Matreier Törl Haus. It is an exciting high-level path without presenting any very great difficulties. It passes near the summits of a series of rock mountains, all over 2500m. The finest situations occur when rounding the SW shoulder of the Vorderer Kendlspitze. The highest point is the Dürrenfeld Scharte (2823m) between the Hinterer Kendlspitze and the Bretterwand Spitze. After this the path drops steeply down crumbly rock, protected with a fixed rope. Then it is easy going over scree and perhaps snow to the delightful Sudetendeutsch Hut with its neighbouring tarn and impressive war memorial crucifix. It also flies a distinctive flag.

The route to the Kleiner and Grosser Muntanitz is known as the Karl Schöttner Weg. East from the hut, you are soon climbing NW on scree and snow above the Gradötz Kees (summer skiing) to the Wellach Köpfe (2962m) at the south end of the Muntanitz ridge. Almost due north along the broad ridge - one of the finest situations in the eastern alps with the Venediger Group to the left and the Glockner to the right. No difficulties along here to the Kleiner, Muntanitz (3192m). This may be journey's end for some walkers. The continuation is down a steep chimney of sandy rock, with a fixed rope: only for those with mountaineering experience, according to the German guidebook, rightly, I think. After this it is an easy slog to the less dramatic, if slightly higher Grosser Muntanitz (3232m). Return to the hut by the same route.

To get back to Matrei go down the steep zig-zag path SW by the Steiner Bach to the Steiner Alm (1909m). From here the official route continues straight down to Lublass on the main road. It is far more pleasant to cross the stream, traverse up round a broad spur and follow an open path across high pastures and down through the woods to Glunz (1447m). Unfortunately the path below Glunz has been largely obliterated in recent years by road building, but it is still possible to find sections of it, and the final stretch is actually signposted.   (1967, 1985)

2.   THE THREE LAKES (DREI SEEN) WALK AND THE FELBER TAUERN (ST. PÖLTENER HUT.)

Scenically the Three Lakes Walk is perhaps the most sheerly beautiful of all

Matrei-based walks, and the Felber Tauern pass is of immense historical interest. There is now also a chair-lift to save the first 500m .steep climb.

By bus or car up the Tauerntal to the Matreier Tauernhaus (1512m). Take the Venedigerblick Chair-lift (built and owned by the same firm, Goldried, that has built the lift to the Panoramaweg - and also a huge hotel in Matrei) up to 2000m. From here NE on a well-used path. After a while you will see on your right the unwardened Grünsee Hut (2235m Cat. I) - the Matrei Section's hut, and soon after the first of the three lakes, the Grünsee (Green Lake) at 2245m, living up to its name if the weather is good. (Note: do not confuse this Grünsee with the Grünsee mentioned in defining the boundaries of the Granatspitze Group.) Keeping left of the lake climb just 100m past a waterfall to the second lake, the Schwarzer See (Black Lake) at 2344m, somewhat more austere than its green neighbour. A rather longer distance and greater climb brings you to the third lake, the Grauer See (Grey Lake) at 2500m, and about 60m above this you reach the Messlingscharte, 2563m. This is a true 'Venedigerblick' with the whole Grosser Venediger massif finely presented.

(To the left of the path rises the Messling Kogel, 2694m, an easy ascent, though scree-ridden at first.)

We turn right, however, and walk NNW almost horizontally on the St. Pöltener Ostweg (East Way). Easy walking, with views to the north soon extending as far as the Kaisergebirge, brings us to the pass known as the Alter (Old) Tauern . The 1937 edition of the Alpenverein, *Venedigergruppe* map shows a projected *motor road* climbing in many hairpin bends from the Matreier Tauernhaus, traversing round nearly to the Alter Tauern, passing under this through a short tunnel and then going past the Obersee and Mittersee and down the Felber Tal to Mittersill. Fortunately for the landscape the Felbertauern Strasse and Tunnel (the main motor road between Munich and Venice) which opened in July 1967 chose the route farther east up the Amer Tal, with a much longer tunnel. This is shown as the projected route even on the Alpenverein's *Granatspitze* map of 1943.

At the Alter Tauern there is a short rocky scramble on to a hog's-back, the Weinbichl. The zig-zag 'path', to the right of a fixed rope over slabs, is the easier way up. The fixed rope seems to be of more help in descent. After going down at the other end of the Weinbichl you are at the Felber Tauern (Neuer Tauern) with the St. Pöltener Hut (2481m Cat. I) opposite. The pass is a stony, snowy, windy, bleak, inhospitable spot, made uglier by a line of electricity pylons. But from prehistoric times until 1967 this had been the easiest pass over the alps at this point. It was used by the Romans, and on the pass is a little belfry, a war memorial, housing a facsimile of the bell which hung here in the Middle Ages to guide travellers in misty weather. There is also a large cross, also a memorial.

(From here the St. Pöltener Westweg - the start of the Venediger Hohenweg - goes to the Neue Prager Hut. A long, hard way.)

We turn south down snow and scree. Keep left when the Westweg turns right. Later, beware of following the route by the Tauernbach - unless indeed you wish to walk all the way into the valley. Otherwise, keep left, climbing a little and you find yourself on a good high-level track high above the Tauerntal with good views up and down the valley, and of the Venediger. This takes you easily back to the top station of the chair-lift. (Take note of the time of the last chair-lift before starting the walk!)   (1984)

XIX: The Glockner Group
(AVE Group 40)

The Name: The Glockner Group takes its name from the Grossglockner, which, at 2798m, is not only the highest in the group, but the highest in Austria. 'Glockner' appears to mean 'bellringer' (which strictly is 'Glöckner'). From the west the mountain has the appearance of a mighty church spire.

There is a 'Glöcknerin' (a female bellringer) in the Radstädter Tauern, but she is only a modest 2432m in height.

Boundaries of the Group: The River Salzach from Uttendorf to Taxenbach - up the Rauriser Tal to Wörth - up the Seidlwinkltal to the Hochtor - down the Tauernbach to its junction with the River Möll - up the Möll to its junction with the Leiterbach - up the Leitertal to the junction with the Moosbach - up the Moosbach to the Peischlachtörl - down the Peischlachbach to Kals - up the Kalserbach and the Dorfertal to the Dorfer See - over the Kalser Tauern to the Weiss See - down the Weissenach to the Grünsee - to Einzinger Boden - and down the Stubachtal to Uttendorf.

Not only does this group contain Austria's highest summit, but it also is the most heavily glaciated mountain group in the country with about 40 glaciers covering altogether an area of approximately 119km². It is therefore an area offering many serious expeditions. The Grossglockner itself is approached from one of two traditionally rival villages, Heiligenblut and Kals. The route described here is based on Kals (no campsite).

Although the Grossglockner by the normal ascent is graded only 1+, it is a serious outing involving glacier-crossing, the use of crampons both on snow and rock and a considerable degree of exposure. For an experienced, roped party, it presents no great problem, but the inexperienced or solitary mountain walker should go with a guide. THE GROSSGLOCKNER IS NOT A WALK IN ANY ORDINARY SENSE OF THE WORD. It is included: because of its popularity and because guides are available.

The routes to the Stüdl Hut that provide the first 'leg' of the

XIX: THE GLOCKNER GROUP

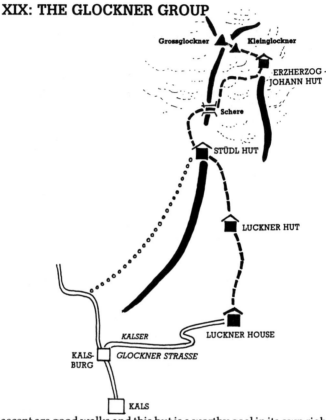

ascent are good walks and this hut is a worthy goal in its own right. Many non-climbers go on to the Erzherzog-Johann Hut on the Adlersruhe, relying on following the guides' beaten tracks over the glacier, but there is risk involved and heavily crevassed areas are all too easily reached if you miss the way.

If you want the services of a guide, go to the 'Bergführer-Vermittlung' in Kals (near the Heimatmuseum). You will be charged a booking-fee of about 20 öS. The guide's own fee depends on the number of clients on his rope. (In 1985 the fee for the Grossglockner normal route, was 2,100 ös for a single client, 1,300 ös each for two and 1,050 ös for three, the normal maximum. If, exceptionally, there were 4 clients the fee fell to 900 ös.) The clients meet their guide at the Stüdl Hut.

1. LUCKNER HOUSE(1984m) - LUCKNER HUT (2227m) STÜDL HUT (2801m) - ERZHERZOG - JOHANN HUT (3454m) - GROSSGLOCKNER (3798m)

Since the opening of the Kalser Glocknerstrasse only the purest, or most impecunious, of purists would walk from Kals to the Luckner House. This fine road climbs from Kals-Burg at about 1300m to the Luckner House at almost 2000m. As a German walker remarked, the toll for a private car of 70 or 80 ös is little more than the shoe leather. If you have no car, or want to return by a different route, the bus also goes to the Luckner House.

From the huge car park near the Luckner House there is a superb, if daunting, view of the Grossglockner. The signposted path from the car park goes up on the right (true left) of the Ködnitzbach, though there is also a rough road on the other side. After a while the road crosses the stream and the path joins it as far as the Luckner Hut, 1hr from the car park. Both the house and hut are private, and, rumour has it, expensive.

Above the Luckner Hut we are on a true mountain path. After a while it crosses the stream and begins to climb more purposefully, but always with good zig-zags and grading. At a fork, keep left for the Stüdl Hut. The path continues to climb below a line of crags until it quite suddenly emerges on the bleak col, the Fanatscharte, where the Stüdl Hut is situated.

Johann Stüdl, one of the principal pioneers of this mountain area, built the original hut here at his own expense in 1868. It is full and busy and obviously very profitable to its wardens, but less friendly and caring than many a less strategically placed hut. (2hrs from the Luckner Hut.)

(If this hut is your goal and you have not left your transport at the Luckner House car park, you may well decide to return to Kals via the Teischnitztal on the west side of the Fanatscharte. This fine route will take you down into the Dorfer Tal about 3km from Kals.)

If you have booked a guide you will meet him here, probably

about 3.00p.m.

The route to the next hut begins due north up a dull, broad, stony shoulder. At the top, turn right and cross the narrow tip of the Teischnitz Glacier to the Schere (3043m), a miniature pass near the southern end of the Luisengrat, a rock ridge named after Stüdl's wife, which leads directly to the steeper Stüdlgrat and so straight to the summit.

The normal route, however, crosses the Schere and continues up the Ködnitz Glacier on the right of the Luisengrat until just below the Luisenkopf (3205m). The route now swings to the right, avoiding crevassed areas: there is a heavily crevassed area now on your left towards the NNW. The glacier steepens until a rock-spur jutting NW from the Blaue Köpfe ridge is reached. You make some height on this, with the protection of fixed ropes in places. Above this, a short convex snow-slope leads to the main rock-ridge which is then followed, with some fixed rope protection for the final 100m or so of height to the hut.

Perched at 3454m on the appropriately named *Adlersruhe* (Eagle's Rest) the Erzherzog-Johann Hut is the highest in the Eastern Alps. It is named after the same Archduke whose name is also borne by the Johannis Hut in the Venediger Group, and was opened in 1880. It can accommodate 220 people but even so is extremely full in the summer season. (If you are with a guide, your sleeping place will be allocated through him.) Although the site and hut (and incidentally a few square metres of the summit, where the cross stands) are owned by the Austrian Alpine *Klub*, not the *Verein* (which we also translate as 'Club') you can get your usual concessions here as an AAC member.

From the hut you will need crampons and a simple shoulder harness, Austrian style, for when you rope up.

The route goes NW up a broad snow shoulder until the snow steepens into what is called the *Glocknerleitl* (presumably the *Glockner Little Ladder*). Up this in steep zig-zags, roping up when the slope really becomes steep. The Glocknerleitl leads to a snow shoulder at the foot of a rock ridge. If you are using an ice-axe, leave it here. The fine ridge is climbed, with fixed ropes in the harder places, to the splendid, narrow summit-ridge of the Kleinglockner, often heavily corniced. Then a 15m drop - excellently protected - to the Obere

Gross Glockner from the Schere

Glocknerscharte dividing the Klein from the Gross. This is crossed on a tiny snow ridge about 8m long and only a few inches wide. Good climbing on sound rock then leads to the Grossglockner summit with its magnificent cross, frequently adorned with dramatically horizontal icicles.

You will be fortunate indeed if your progress is as continuous as this description implies! The queue on the Kleinglockner can easily resemble a supermarket check-out, especially if the Austrian army is practising mountain warfare.

The descent is by the same route. Do not underestimate the terrain *below* the top hut. When you reach the rock spur near the top of the glacier you may find it better (or your guide may) to keep right of it and go straight down steep snow. (1985)

(Apparently it is possible, if you go with a guide, to get a certificate that you have climbed this mountain!)

173

XX: The Schober Group
(AVE Group 41)

Boundaries of the Group: R. Möll from junction with the Leiterbach to Winklern - Iselsberg - Iseltal from Lienz to Huben - Kalser Bach to Kals - Ködnitzbach - Peischlachbach - Peischlachtörl - Moosbach - Leiterbach to junction with Möll.

This group takes its name from its highest top, the Hochschober (3242m). It is well served with huts. Possible bases are Kals in the NW and Heiligenblut in the NE, though in mountaineering terms these are both normally regarded as bases for the Großglockner. For most purposes the best base in Lienz, whence a drivable road gives easy access almost to the Lienzer Hut in the heart of the group.

Lienz is also the base for the Villgratner Group (XVII - AVE Group 38) and the Lienz Dolomites in the Gailtaler Alpen (XXV, AVE Group 56).

Strategically and touristically placed at the junction of the Drau with its much larger tributary, the Isel, this town boasts an ancient and continuous history at least from the 1st century AD, when a Roman settlement - the only Roman town in the Tirol - was established at Aguntum or Aguntinum about 3m/5km east of Lienz: an excavated site with museum that is well worth a visit, as is Lavant, about 3km due south of it. To walk up the hill past the Stations of the Cross is also to move through history, past Roman, early Christian to Gothic architecture. In the town itself history through later centuries is constantly before your eyes. There is plenty of accommodation in Lienz and two campsites, the Campsite Falkner not far from the stadium (looked crowded) and the Seewiese Campsite by the Tristacher See (826m). As the lake is the town's open-air swimming pool there is a free bus between the town and the campsite! The site is beautifully situated, well run, with first class facilities, though obviously not cheap. As you look from the campsite along the lake you see the Hochstein Hut and beyond it the Böses Weibele (see XVII, Villgratner Group), while from the restaurant terrace just above the campsite you can pick out the Untere Seescharte on the way to the Wangenitzsee Hut (see Walk 2).

1. THE NEUALPL LAKES (c.2430m)

The Lienz winter skiing playground on the Zettersfeld is reached by gondola-lift to 1812m followed by a four-seater chair-lift to 2200m where there is a restaurant and from where the paragliders launch themselves into space.

Take Route 9 (AV Path 913). After less than 1km there is a signpost at a fork.

(The best route now is to fork left to pass the Goiselemandl (2433m) on its SW slopes. Continue on a quite sharp but not difficult ridge to the next signpost, and thence fork right down to the lakes.)

The alternative (which in any case also provides a good return route) is to fork right at the first signpost. A broad and well made path, steep in one place, goes directly to the group of Neualpl Lakes, two larger, four smaller, a picturesque setting with fine views. On the way you will have passed near a stone table marked 'Stammtisch' on the map, jocularly referring to the name of the special table in Austrian and German inns reserved for a special group of regular customers.

Potter at will among the lakes and return by the path on the north side of the Goiselemandl.   (1995)

(For a longer trip, continuation to the Sattelkopf (2651m) is suggested in the local brochure. It involves an additional 200m ascent and descent and is not shown on maps as a waymarked path.)

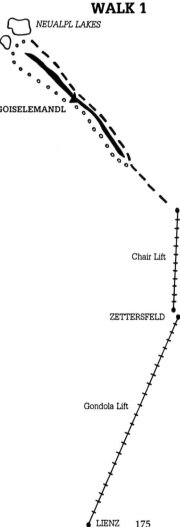

XX: SCHOBER GROUP WALK 1

NEUALPL LAKES

GOISELEMANDL

Chair Lift

ZETTERSFELD

Gondola Lift

LIENZ   175

2. LIENZER HUT (1977m) and WANGENITZSEE HUT (2508m) (3 days)

Route: Seichenbrunn (1686m) - Gaimberg Alm (1753m) - Lienzer Hut (1977m) - Untere Seescharte (2593m) - Wangenitzsee Hut (2508m) - Untere Seescharte - Seichenbrunn.

This satisfying and beautiful walk starts at Seichenbrunn in the Debant Tal. If you have transport, use it to reach this! Take the Heiligenblut road out of Lienz past Debant. Beyond Göriach after a tight double bend, turn off left at an acute angle by a bus stop near the Gasthof Moserbach on to a narrow, rough road. After 2km or so at a sawmill and guest-house (In der Sag) this road crosses the river and is joined by a road coming up from Unternußdorf. Soon you cross the river again (1185m) and the valley-base opens out somewhat until after another 6km, approximately, Seichenbrunn is reached. Here at the end of the public road there is an unexpectedly large car park, the valley station of the goods cable-way to the Wangenitzsee Hut and the boundary sign of the 'AUSSENZONE' (outer zone) of the Tauern National Park. There is a sign for the Wangenitzsee Tal. This is the way (Path 917) you will return at the end of the walk. There is also a sign for the Lienzer Hut via the "Gaimberger Feld". Don't be misled by this: the route involves an ascent of nearly 700m and takes you half way to the Wangenitzsee Hut. Instead choose either the road or the Nature Trail (Lehrpfad). These virtually meet at the Gaimberg Alm (1753m), the nature trail keeping to its right, near the river, and the road keeping to its left. (You can change from the one to the other here.) Less than 2km beyond the alm and 200m higher you reach the Lienzer Hut - a pleasant and busy hut with its own electricity, and flush toilets.

(An entirely different way to reach this hut from Lienz is to take the Zetterfeld gondola-lift, walk up to the youth hostel and then take the Lienzer Höhenweg all the way to the hut.)

Next morning, drop down to the river and follow Path 917 (NOT the nature trail and NOT 915). At about 2000m you encounter a rough, steep section that circumvents the Schalbenwand. There follows a long (over 2km) section, the Zinkeweg, that contours above the Gaimberger Feld to reach a path junction with a bold sign painted on a rock:

<— L.H.   W.H. —>
TAL

"TAL" (valley) is the path against which you have been warned as a route to the Lienzer Hut but which you will use for the return to Seichenbrunn. For now, continue towards WH (Wangenitzsee Hut). The path begins to climb round the foot of the dramatic cliffs of the Feldkopf, then in steep zig-zags for the final 130m or so of height to the Untere Seescharte (2593m) where a gantry carries the cable-way over the top. This is one of those 'magic moments' in the mountains. Suddenly you see a huge basin, with the Kreuzsee (2483m) and the Wangenitz See (2465m), and with the hut standing up beyond them, some 50m higher than the lower lake. Go down from the pass and cross the isthmus between the lakes and so up to the hut: a splendid hut, finely situated.

For the return, go back over the Untere Seescharte and as far as the painted boulder, then down (TAL), at first over high pastures to about 2100m, then more steeply for two or three hundred metres loss of height, and finally through woods back to the car park.

(1995)

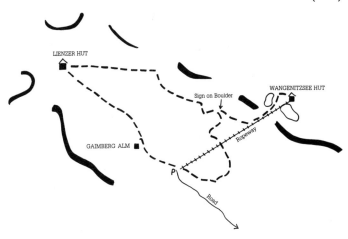

XX: SCHOBER GROUP WALK 2

XXI: The Goldberg Group
(AVE Group 42)
&
XXII: The Ankogel Group
(AVE Group 44)

Boundaries of the Groups

GOLDBERG: Salzach from Taxenbach to junction with Gasteiner Ache - Gasteiner Ache - Naßfeld - Niederer Tauern - Mallnitzbach - to its junction with the Möll - the Mölltal to Heiligenblut - Tauernbach - Hochtor - Seidwinkltal - Rauriser Tal - Taxenbach.

ANKOGEL: The Salzach from junction with the Gasteiner Ache to the junction with the Großarlbach - Großarlbach to the junction with the Kreealpenbach - Murtörl - the Mur to St Michael - Klausgraben - Katschberghöhe - Katschbach - Lieser to junction with the Drau - Drau to junction with the Möll - Mölltal to junction with the Mallnitzbach - Mallnitzbach - Niederer Tauern - Gasteiner Ache to its junction with the Salzach.

The walks described here are based on the Gastein Valley and thus all on the eastern side of the Goldberg Group and the western edge of the Ankogel Group.

As the name of the Goldberg Group implies the mountains are rich in minerals, and the political power of the Salzburg Archbishopric was formerly grounded on the copper, silver, gold and salt mines which had been exploited even by the Romans who also valued the supposed healing properties of certain springs. A hospice with baths, founded by a mine-owner in 1489 still exists. It became so famous that even the legendary doctor Paracelsus visited it. Because (or in spite!) of the fact that the water of the Gastein Stollen contains radon it is visited for medicinal purposes even today.

Badgastein is built on a huge natural amphitheatre where the river, the Gasteiner Ache, thunders down through the very midst of the town from its upper reaches at some 1000m above sea level to the lower valley towards Bad Hofgastein some 200m lower down. The

XXI: THE GOLDBERG GROUP
XXII: THE ANKOGEL GROUP

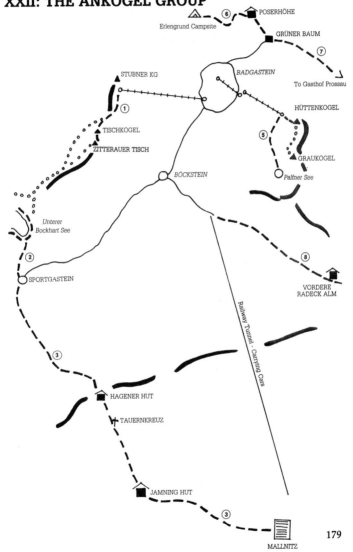

179

campsites, of which the Erlengrund, though not cheap, is highly to be recommended, lie in the lower valley. Bad Hofgastein is a pleasing and well laid out spa town, the special waters having been conducted there by pipe line.

The Ankogel Group is dominated by the Ankogel itself (3246m) and its associated summits and glaciers and is penetrated on the Gastein side by two exceptionally beautiful valleys, the Kötschachtal and the Anlauftal.

1. THE ZITTERAUER TISCH (2463m) TISCHKOGEL (2409m) AND THE STUBNERKOGEL (2246m).

Route: From the summit station of the Stubnerkogel Gondelbahn - north - Stubnerkogel. South and SW - Zitterauer Scharte (2163m) - Tischkogel (2409m) - Zitterauer Tisch (2463m).

Start at the summit station of the Stubnerkogel Gondelbahn. (Masochists and purists may reach this on Path 111 from the bottom station: the climb is of about 1200m!) The Stubnerkogel is a few yards to the north and barely worth a visit unless, like me, you are a 'summit bagger'. The view is as good from the terrace of the restaurant: and there is beer there, too.

For the real walks follow the ridge south and then SW down to the Zitterauer Scharte (2163m) where a chair-lift comes up from the Angertal side. Then climb steeply - almost a scramble - to the cross on the Tischkogel (2409m)

(Where the steeper section begins, a fork to the right leads to the Otto Reichert Way, a well-made, almost level path that by-passes the Zitterauer Tisch on the west side and after crossing the Miesbichlscharte (2237m) drops down to the Unterer Bockhart See (see Walk 2), a fork giving the choice of the NW or SE end of the lake, and thus to Sportgastein: bus)

From the Tischkogel it is a mere grassy stroll to the Zitterauer Tisch (2463m). To the north you can see the Hoch König, and down in the deep valley to the SE is the clinic at the mouth of the tunnel that carries the thermal waters.

(It is possible to continue SW to join the Otto Reicher way.

There is also an alternative route to the Tischkogel reached by forking left at the Zitterauer Scharte and then right up a steep arête. The signpost claims that that is the easier way. It is also possible to go down, either from the Tischkogel direct (steep), or from the Zitterauer Scharte to the Obere

Zitterauer Alm and then to walk on a road to the middle station of the Gondelbahn.)

(1994)

2. UNTERER BOCKHART SEE (1872m)

Route: Sportgastein (1589m) - Bockhartsee Hut (1933m) - Unterer Bockhart See (1872m).

The Bockhart See, mentioned in Walk 1 is also worth visiting in its own right.

Start at Sportgastein, a ski development in the Naßfeld valley area. You can drive to this up the valley of the Naßfelder Ache above Bockstein on a modern road, the Gasteiner Alpenstraße, through a fantastic series of tunnels. (Toll at the Gasteiner Heilstollen.) There is also a bus from Badgastein (toll included in the fare).

(Sportgastein can also be reached on foot on the Naßfelder Wanderweg from Bockstein.)

The normal way up follows a road past an old hospice, but this eventually leads to a closed tunnel with a locked gate and not open to the public; so from this point you follow the old, original path that pre-dates the road, which was evidently built in connection with the hydro-electric waterworks. It is not easy to find the start of this path at valley level, but on return you can follow it down fairly easily and thus avoid some road walking.

In about an hour from Sportgastein you reach the privately run Bockhartsee Hut (1933m) where you can sit outside with a view of the lake before walking down and crossing the dam. From the dam do NOT take a steep track down to the right. It is dangerous, does not give access to the valley, and is evidently in connection with the hydro-electric power station below. At the far end of the dam a path comes down from the Miesbichlscharte (see Walk 1). Do not follow this but keep left on the lakeside path - very beautiful, a nature reserve where fishing is prohibited. At the end of the lake bear left and climb almost pathlessly until you meet a very good path, the Herrensteig. Go left on this to return to the dam. (Round the lake, about 1¹/₂hrs.)

(If you turned right on the Herrensteig you would reach the smaller Oberer Bockhartsee (2076m) or could fork right on the Zimburg Way to the Miesbichlscharte (see Walk 1).)

You can by-pass the hut (indeed you could have done so in ascent) and go down the path as already described. (1994)

3. THE HAGENER HUT (2448m), THE JAMNING HUT (1745m) AND MALLNITZ (2 days).

Route: Sportgastein - Eselkar - Niedere Tauern (Mallnitzer Tauern) and Hagener Hut (2448m) - Tauernhaus - Tauernkreus - Jamning Hut (1745m) - Mallnitz.

Start at Sportgastein (see Walk 2: but don't drive here to park. You are not returning here). Walk south through the wide, level valley on good farm roads for about 40mins to the foot of steep zig-zags that climb over 400m in 1km on the map! (Beware of going left on the Weißenbachtal path.) You will be glad of a rest in the tiny hut at the top of the zig-zags (2099m). You are still some 350m below the Hagener Hut, but the rest of the route is less demanding: primarily a big clockwise rising traverse round a big basin, the Eselkar. You may find a little snow here even in high summer.

At the pass itself, a few metres below the hut, there is a bell, as at the St. Pöltener Hut near Matrei, for this pass, like that one, is one of the most ancient passes over the eastern alps, having been used from Roman and pre-Roman times up to 1911, when the Tauern Railway Tunnel was opened.

The hut, built in 1912, stands proudly on the bleak pass, which lies not only on the boundary between the Goldberg and Ankogel mountain groups, but also on that between the states of Salzburg and Kärnten (Carinthia). It is a busy hut, for it is also on the high-level route from the Ankogel to the Hoher Sonnblick and is within the Hoher Tauern National Park.

Be sure to follow the correct path down to Mallnitz!

A little way down you will find the Tauernhaus, substantially built early in the 20th century but then neglected. In 1945 the final blow was given to it when British soldiers, who had a temporary barrack on the pass, used the roof timbers for firewood. It was later taken over by the Alpenverein who have restored it and provided an exhibition about its history.

The next feature of interest is the Tauernkreuz (2235m), standing on a bare and seemingly undramatic spot. The inscription of the cross reads (in translation): *On this spot Frau Theresia Angermann, for many years warden of the Hagener Hut, was killed by lightning on 18 July 1949. Walker, think of her. RIP.*

The route now drops more steeply for some 400m of height, in wide zig-zags on the broad spur between the Tauernbach and the Laschgbach. The Jamning Hut (1745m) commands a fine view all the way down the Tauerntal to Mallnitz. A public road from Mallnitz on the north side (true left) of the valley leads to a car park and bus terminus just below the hut, but on the south side (true right) a lovely path keeps remote from traffic, steeply at first, then along level meadows and woods (2¹/₂hrs to Mallnitz).

The most practical way of returning to Bad Gastein is to take the train through the Tauern Tunnel. This 8552m-long tunnel was opened in 1911 after long and bitter disputes as to the route for a north-south railway tunnel through the mountains. Out of no fewer than ten possibilities which were considered by the Vienna Government the choice was finally narrowed to Gmünd or Gastein. In 1901 the Emperor Franz Josef opted for the Gastein route, and the actual tunnelling, which involved removing 1.6 million cubic metres of hard granite, was completed in six years. Although it is purely a railway tunnel it provides a through route for road traffic. Cars are loaded on specially designed trains at Böckstein and Mallnitz.

(1994)

4. MAUSKARKOPF (2373m) AND HIRSCHKARSPITZE (2119m).

Route: Kleine Scharte (2050m) - Mauskarkopf (2373m) - Hirschkarspitze (2119m) - Klein Scharte.

From Bad Hofgastein to the Kleine Scharte Mountain Restaurant the difference in height is about 1100m. It may be easily reached by using the Schloßalmbahn: stage 1, a train (standing only) on rails to about 1300m, then a gondola-lift to the top. Almost immediately you will see a signpost to the Mauskarkopf. This is not the red waymarked route but has much to commend it, especially going up. It leads to a little col. From this the summit cone is steep, loose at

XXI: GOLDBERG GROUP
WALK 4

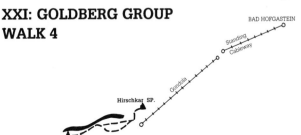

first, then with a fixed rope and then gradually easier until the cross on the lovely, tiny summit comes into sight. Super views from the top.

On the way down do not go right at the little col but continue directly towards the Hirschkarspitze. This is the red waymarked route. There is a very steep section, short but nasty.

The much eroded path up the Hirschkarspitze is easy, but the mountain itself, really a rocky spur, is justly celebrated as one of the finest viewpoints in the Gastein Valley. Seats near the cross encourage a long contemplative rest.

No problem to return to Kleine Scharte.   (1994)

5. THE HÜTTENKOGEL (2231m) AND THE PALFNER SEE (2074m).

Route: Graukogelbahn (top station) - Hüttenkogel (2231m) - Graukogelbahn, top station (near) - Palfner See (2074m) - Graukogelbahn.

Except for the descent from the Hagener Hut to Mallnitz, Walks 1-4 are all on the Goldberg side of the Gastein valley. Walks 5-8 are all on the edge of the Ankogel Group.

A striking feature of the view from the Erlengrund Campsite and its environs is the ridge to the SE that rises from the Hüttenkogel at its northern end to the Graukogel (2492m) at its southern end.

The Graukogelbahn's valley station is on the road from the town to Grüner Baum (see Walks 6 & 7). It is in two stages, the first a single chair-lift, the second a double. Despite its name it ends about 280m below the Hüttenkogel, which is reached by a well-graded zig-zag path: an easy and rewarding walk to what is a fine viewpoint. Notice the Reedsee exactly 400m below in the forest, and the Tischlerkarkopf (3002m) and Tischlerkar Glacier beyond. There is a stone-built shelter and a cross with a 'conservationist' text from Revelation Chap. 14 v 7: *Fear God and give him the glory,* followed by a lame verse, which translates: *O Father, let thy world still exist and do not let the beauty of the Creation die. Instead of destroying we wish to glorify.*

(A more exciting walk would be to follow the path along the ridge. There are fixed ropes across a small gap before the route finally goes up without difficulty on open slopes to the summit of the Graukogel.)

For the walk described here, go down again almost to the top station of the chair-lift, then left on Path 527, which contours almost level above the forest line with a good view across the valley to the Stubnerkogel-Tischkogel ridge (see Walk 1). After a time it bears left with steeper grass below. At a fork do not follow 527 (right) down to the ruined Palfner Hochalm, but keep left, climbing quite steeply on a much rougher path until the beautiful Palfner See comes into view under its glorious cirque of precipitous summits, of which the highest, the Palfner Seekogel, reaches 2531m.

(The path continues due east and climbs almost 300m to the lowest point of the cirque, the Palfner Scharte (2321m). From here it drops 500m to the Reedsee and a further 700m into the Kötschachtal (see Walk 7). Alternatively turn left (due north) and climb a further 170m up the narrow ridge to the summit of the Graukogel. There is no proper path and this route is only for experienced mountain walkers. For the Hüttenkogel and Graukogelbahn reverse the route described earlier.)

For the present walk return to the Graukogelbahn top station and restaurant by reversing the way you have come.   (1994)

6. THE POSERHÖHE (1505m).

Route: Erlengrund (c.850m) - Gasthof Gamskar (Ardackerbahn Bridge) - Gasthof Poserhöhe - Grüner Baum (1066m) - Erlengrund. The usual ascent is from Grüner Baum. The route given here makes a round walk, but the way up is not signposted until near the end, so careful map-reading is called for. (Try to get the 1:25,000 *Gasteiner Wanderkarte* published locally. It is much clearer to follow than the *Kompass 1:50,000.*)

If starting from Erlengrund, pass the Reithalle and walk up the road towards Grüner Baum. Ignore a fork that drops to the right and take the second turning left. A tractor track on the right climbs fairly gently and meets the way up from the bridge by the Gasthof Gamskar. If you miss the first track go on to the bridge and take the path there: steeper and shorter than the other. Although apparently used by tractors the path is steep and quite dramatic, with occasional rewarding glimpses of the valley below. Eventually, at a clearing (open pastures) the track goes straight on to an alm building, while the path goes sharp left. Signpost: *Poserhöhe 15 Minutes* - optimistic, but at least a 'real' path.

The Gasthof Poserhöhe is a lovely hut with a couple of entertaining wooden figures and a superb view of Bad Gastein. Indeed, this view has been used as the cover of the local publicity brochure.

Go down on the Luis Trenker Way to Grüner Baum. This is much steeper than the route up suggested here, and there are many comic notices obviously designed to persuade people not to give up. (e.g. *Sei nicht dumm, kehrt nicht um: Don't be stupid, don't turn back.*) A large notice at the bottom says One Hour! No wonder visitors need the comic notices! The local guidebook is rather more realistic with 1¹/₂hrs.

Return by road. Start on the main road (bus route) towards the town but soon turn off, right, down a minor road which soon proves to be the road on which you started up. (1994)

7. THE KÖTSCHACHTAL AND PROSSAU.

The last two walks in this section are not strictly mountain walks, but as they both penetrate into magnificent valley heads of the Ankogel Group, they do merit inclusion.

Route: Grüner Baum - Himmelwand (1086m) - Hintere Prossau - Gasthaus Prossau (1271m).

"Grüner Baum" (Green Tree) is a hotel-hamlet at the lower end of the Kötschachtal with car parks and a bus terminus. The nearby *Malerwinkel* (Artists' Corner) is said to be world-famous. Many people might share the opinion that despite a good view up the valley its picturesqueness is over-rated. A curiosity here is a sort of shrine put here by Luis Trenker, who also gave his name to the path from here to the Poserhöhe. This 'shrine' contains a 'book' whose 'pages' are made of copper and are engraved with the name of every person killed by accident in this valley during the 20th century. Included are fourteen (I think) people who were killed with all their stock in the early 1950s by an avalanche 20m deep. There is a special memorial to these further up the valley.

Ahead of you all the way is the Böchstein Kogel (2527m), apparently a free-standing pyramid but actually the end of a vast horseshoe.

In about 1km you pass the Gasthof Himmelwand (Wall of Heaven) just below a cliff of the same name. Perhaps it is better to visit this on the return journey! Just over 1km further, at point 1117, there is a footbridge on the right and a sign to the Reedsee at 1831. Two kilometres further the Gasthaus Prossau comes into view on the left. Leave it for the moment and turn right up a rough track to Hintere Prossau and the true valley-head (Talschluß), a cirque almost comparable with the celebrated Cirque de Gavarnie in the French Pyrenees. Many glacier-fed waterfalls pour down its walls. It is worth pressing on beyond the track in order to relish the full savour of the place.

Now you may return to the picturesque and hospitable Gasthaus Prossau: its *Prossauerteller* is excellent. And you've no doubt earned a drink at the Himmelwand as well.   (1994)

8. THE ANLAUFTAL AND RADECK ALM.

Route: Bahnhof Böckstein (railway station 1172m) - Marienstein (1200m) -Bridge (1318m) - Junction with path to Korntauern (1347m) - Vordere Radeck Alm (1578m) - Hintere Radeck Alm (ruin 1709m) - end of path near river junction.

Start near Böckstein Railway Station where cars are loaded for the Tauerntunnel. Pass a few houses and the Marienstein and you are in the National Park. The valley is beautiful and the rock scenery dramatic. You cross the Anlaufbach on a stone bridge at 1318m, and at 1347m notice a footbridge and a path to the right.

(This climbs to the Korntauern (Hoher Tauern, 2459m), a pass over which it is possible to reach Mallnitz, though less easily than over the Niederer Tauern (2448m) where the Hagener Hut lies.)

About 2km beyond this you reach the Vordere Radeck Alm, a charming place with good food, beer kept cool in an open-air tank of running mountain water, and loos where your droppings really do drop, too far below to be offensive. Sitting outside the house you can look right up the valley to the Ankogel itself (3246m)

To the ruined Hintere Radeck Alm (1709m) the path is rougher and steeper. The waymarked path ends here, but you can continue more level by the river on a stony 'made' path up and down which cattle can evidently be driven, for you may see them grazing on the open pastures towards the wild and spacious valley head. (Return the same way.)   (1994)

XXIII: The Radstädter Tauern
(AVE Group 45a)

The Name: The name 'Tauern' has long been applied to a vast area of the Central Eastern Alps from the Venediger Group in the west to the junction of the R. Mur with the Liesingbach in the east. The western part, comprising nine separate mountain groups, including the Venediger, Granatspitz and Glockner Groups, has been and still is known to mountaineers as the Hohe (High) Tauern. East of this there used to be a 'giant group' with the umbrella title 'Niedere Tauern' (Low Tauern), which climbers and guidebooks variously divided into arbitrary groups. Now (1984) the Alpenverein has divided the Niedere Tauern into four clearly defined groups (45 a, b, c & d) of which the Radstädter Tauern (45a, named from the town of Radstadt) is the most westerly.

The adjacent group to the east of the Radstädter Tauern, the Schladminger Tauern (45b, named from the town of Schladming) is continuous with it and the two sections should be read in conjunction. Some walkers will decide to make a single walk covering both groups from east to west or vice versa: E-W has the advantage that you are looking towards the glaciated snow peaks of the Hohe Tauern; W-E the advantage that the country through which you walk becomes steadily more beautiful.

Boundaries of the Group: The Wagrainer Bach from its junction with the Salzach - the Wagrainer Hohe - the Litzlingbach to its junction with the Enns - the Enns to Radstadt - the northern Taurachtal - Obertauern - the southern Taurachtal - Mautendorf - Neusess - Mur - Murtörl - Kreealpenbach - Grossarlbach to its junction with the Salzach - the Salzach to its junction with the Wagrainerbach.

Radstadt, the base for the walks described here, is most easily reached by using the Salzburg-Klagenfurt motorway. Though it has interesting fortifications it is not a particularly attractive town. The campsite, though it has good facilities, is on clay soil and very near the main road to the Balkans, and therefore much used by

XXIII: THE RADSTÄDTER TAUERN WALKS 1-4

overnighters.

The walks described will be based on the Südwiener (South Vienna) Hut, plus an additional shortish walk to a splendid viewpoint in the Salzburger Schieferalpen north of the town. Another walk based on Radstadt will be described in the Schladminger Tauern section.

1. TO THE SÜDWIENER HUT (1802m Cat. I)

a) Via the Wildseesteig, a section of the Tauernhohenweg long distance footpath

By bus or car to Obertauern at the Tauern Pass, the watershed between the northern and southern Taurach Valleys. It is a harsh, commercially developed ski-resort. There is a large and important hut here, however, the DAV-Haus Obertauern (1738m Cat. II)

189

which you may well use as your base if you are not camping. And only ¹/₂hr walk on the east (Schladminger Tauern) side is the equally large Seekarhaus (1797m Cat. II) - also accessible by mini bus. The paths in the immediate vicinity of Obertauern have been confused by ski-developments, and the whole eastern side of the Gamsspitzel (2348m), the mountain immediately to its west, has been smoothed out to create piste. This has spoiled the walk up (there is a cable-car, too), though the view from it is good. Do not climb this to reach the hut, however. The hut path is more to the right (north). It is wild and beautiful, traversing the northern slopes of the Gamsspitzel (under the cable of the lift), then a little SW until you reach the Wildsee (1925m) lying mere-like below the Teufelshörner (2262m) and the Glöcknerin (2432m). A locked-up private hut here has the 'Wildsee' rubber stamp in a box outside.

Just before you reach the Wildsee, notice a path to the right: this leads steeply down to the Hirschwandsteig (Walk 1b) and beyond that to the Felseralm (1660m) and the main road in the northern Taurachtal.

The Wildseesteig, however, continues west, climbing to a nameless col and then higher to the Hirschwandsattel. Beyond this again the path crosses an elevation (scarcely a hill) called Hengst ('The Stallion', 2074m), with fine views to the Pleisslingkeil in the south and the Steinfeldspitze in the north-west, and then falls gently to 1926m, turns sharply north and soon reaches the hut.

Built in 1928, this is a traditional mountain chalet of dark wood. In 1978 - its 50th anniversary - it had very friendly wardens.

(1978 + Information 1982)

b) Via the Hirschwandsteig

This pleasant path is more or less parallel with the Wildseesteig but rather lower, say 200m, still a high path. From the Tauern Pass walk down (path) to the Fluhbachalm - or start from there (bus stop). Follow the track west almost to the Neuhofalm (1650m) and continue on the marked path, crossing the path from the Wildsee to the Felseralm (1660m) and so to the hut. A good way to return to Obertauern if you went by route 1a.
(1978)

(c) You may drive from Gnadenbrückl (1226m), on the main road

in the northern Taurachtal, to the Gnaden Alm (1326m, car park) and from there walk up to the hut. This is the shortest route: 1¹/₂hrs.

d) There is also a toll road all the way to the hut from Flachau in the Flachautal!)

2. THE STEINFELDSPITZE (2344m)

An elegant mountain and excellent viewpoint.

Leave the Südwiener Hut by the toll road, west. This swings in an arc clockwise. At a sharp bend just before reaching the Hafeicht Alm and Chapel continue on a path NE to the Hafeicht Scharte (1335m). Turn north here, leaving the main path, and follow red waymarks until you finally scramble on to a fine limestone ridge between the Steinfeldspitze and the K1. Bärenstaffl (2014m). To the north you suddenly gain a view down the Zauch valley, with the Zauch See and many guest-houses - a popular ski area. Turn left (west) on the ridge. It is airy, and there is one 'bad step' before the easy walk up to the summit cross. More views!   (1978)

3. THE GROSSER PLEISSLINGKEIL (2501m), THE GROSSWAND (2436m) AND THE GLÖCKNERIN (2432m).

These three summits, combined with a return via the Wildseesteig, offer a glorious day's round.

Leave the hut as if for the Wildseesteig, but just before Hengst (2074m) fork right (SE), delightfully through latschen fields and high pastures towards the Pliesslingkeil, which is climbed on some what monotonous scree-slopes. Pause sometimes to look north at the marvellous symmetry of the Steinfeldspitze in the middle distance and the Dachstein massif some 25 to 30km away. The summit view extends to the glaciated peaks of the Hohe Tauern to the SW. South, the mountain falls into the Lantschefeldbach valley. Due east is the ridge which is your route.

A steep and loose descent leads to easier ground and an excellent path, almost on the ridge, towards the Grosswand (2436m), in some ways an even better viewpoint. Now SE easily to the Glöcknerin, walking on the very crest of the ridge. From the Glöcknerin superb views: our 'own' ridge to the west, the Dachstein to the north, the Hochfeind (2689m) across the deep valley to the south, and to the

Pleißlingkeil from Großwand

east the rest of the ridge and, away beyond the Tauern Pass, the Schladminger Tauern, dominated by the fin-like shape of the Hochgolling (2863m).

Return from the Glöcknerin to the main ridge and pick up the route leading down towards a boulder field on the rim of the basin in which lies the Wildsee. Do not go down to the lake, but traverse the basin on its western side until you meet the Wildseesteig. Back to the hut on this as Walk 1a.   (1978)

4. THE TAFERLSCHARTE (2236m)

The Tauristia Hut that used to lie at the very head of the Flachautal at 1195m has been sacrificed to the motorway, which enters a tunnel at that point, so the next hut westerly from the Südwiener Hut is the Franz-Fischer Hut (2020m. Cat. I) some 5½-7 hours away and the base for the popular Mosermandl (2680m). The walk described here is the start of that route.

From the Südwiener Hut, south to a little grassy saddle, from here along the west side of the Höllkogel (2210m). This is not worth climbing: its horrible pathless limestone scree justifies its name

'Hell-dome'. Then climb gently on bare country (the Windfeld 'Wind-field') marred by pylons and huge metal snow-breaks to defend these. This is also the pass from the Pleisslingtal to the Landschefeldtal. Continue on a broad ridge to the Taferlscharte.

(1978)

(From here the path drops steeply to the south, either straight down to Wald in the Zederhaustal, or swinging west to the Franz-Fischer Hut.

There should also be a fairly easy ridge-walk over the stony summits SE of the pass (the Stampferwand etc.) if the waymarks have been renewed in recent years. If not, be careful, as it is rough ground.)

5. ROSSBRAND (1770m) (An additional walk from Radstadt).

This walk does not actually belong to the Radstädter Tauern but is on the edge of the Salzburger Schieferalpen (AVE Group 12) north of the River Enns. However, it is a walk to be undertaken from Radstadt and its splendid views include a panorama of the Radstädter Tauern.

The path goes up almost from the campsite. There is no need to follow the zig-zagging forestry road: use Footpath 462. About 300m up you may enjoy coffee - and perhaps Apfelstrudel as well - at the Bürgerberg Alm (1170m). From here it is exactly 600m to the summit, with fabulous views of the Niedere Tauern and the Dachstein massif, with the Bischofsmütze and the Gosaukamm. A walk along the broad 'ridge' is worth having before going down, either the same way or on 461 via Rohrmoos: but this does finish on a forestry road. (1978)

SALZBURGER SCHIEFERALPEN

ADDITIONAL WALK FROM RADSTADT

XXIV: The Schladminger Tauern
(AVE Group 45b)

The Name: See under *Radstädter Tauern*
Boundaries of the Group: The R. Enns from Radstädt to the
junction with the Gross-sölkbach - the Gross-sölkbach - the Sölker
Pass - the Katschbach to its junction with the R. Mur - the R. Mur to
Oberbaierndorf - Neusess - Mautendorf - the southern Taurachtal
Obertauern - the northern Taurachtal - Radstädt.

This is one of the most beautiful and unspoilt areas in the Austrian
Alps and would be the heart of the projected Niedere Tauern
National Park It has no through roads or railways north-south or
east-west; ski-developments are limited to its very edges, and it is
still free of hydro-electric vandalism.

The area .covers some 500sq. kms of virtually undeveloped,
untouched mountain landscape with more than 230 summits of
over 2000m, 150 waterfalls and over 300 lakes and tarns, about 40 of
them in the Klafferkessel (roughly 'The Gaping Cauldron'), the
area's most extraordinary natural feature, nearly 2km across, up to
300m deep on the S and SW, but tipped towards the north like a
giant crucible being emptied into the valley. The rocks of the
Schladminger Tauern are richly and variously coloured, warm red
predominating.

The main Schladminger Tauern Range lies south of Schladming
(accommodation. campsite), and forms a shapely crescent whose
horns point north. Its traverse from Obertauern to the Bodensee in
the Seewigtal needs a minimum of about 5 days. The walk can also
be broken into sections and several picturesque approach valleys
explored. The first recorded climb of the Hochgolling (2863m), the
highest mountain in the group, was by an unknown climber in 1791,
by a route now rarely used. In 1885 the Preintaler Club was founded
and the area was thoroughly explored between this date and the
First World War, primarily by Hans Wödl, a member of the Club.

The main high-level traverse path will be described in sections,
so that approach valleys can be included, but the reader can easily

XXIV: THE SCHLADMINGER TAUERN WEST-EAST TRAVERSE

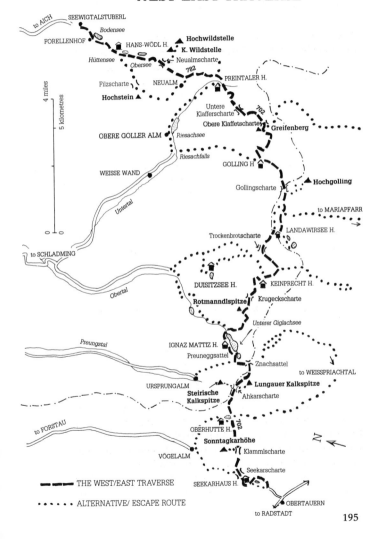

—— THE WEST/EAST TRAVERSE

• • • • • ALTERNATIVE/ ESCAPE ROUTE

link these into a continuous trip, which constitutes the finest unglaciated walk of its length in the Austrian Alps.

1. OBERTAUERN TO IGNAZ-MATTIS HUT (1986m)

The walk starts at Obertauern, an ugly skiing development at the Tauern Pass on the road from Radstadt to Mautendorf. You can start from the DAV-Haus Obertauern (1738m. Cat. II), an austere building of 1969/70 on the main road, or from the Seekarhaus (1797m). This is about 2km NE of the Pass - past the Tennis Hall. You can drive to it and park there if you are staying. It is a comfortable hut originally belonging to the former copper-mines and was rescued from ruin in the 1920s by the Austria Section of the Alpenverein. It is now privately owned.

Pleasant though the hut is, it is good to get moving away from the ski-scars of Obertauern, though actually the first waymark after you leave the hut is on a ski-pylon. Then the walking is pleasant up to the Seekarscharte (2010m) where you finally take leave of Obertauern.

You can also reach this point up the Forstautal from Forstau in the Enns Valley, but if you *drive* up to the Vögel Alm (at own risk) you will later have a problem to rejoin your car.

You are now on the Tauernhohenweg (Tauern High Level Path) No.702, which leads delightfully through hillocky country interspersed with tarns and outcrops, to the Klammlscharte. From here you may ascend the Sonntagkar-Höhe (2245m), due north, pathlessly but without difficulty, if you feel confident enough to make a detour so early in the day for the sake of good views. Now down to the Oberhüttensattel (1866m) above the charming Oberhütten See. At the Oberhütte it is possible to obtain refreshments. You could also reach this saddle from the Forstautal and the Vögel Alm.

You must now climb nearly 500m to the Ahkarscharte (2315m) between the Steirische Kalkspitze (2459m) to the north, and the Lungauer Kalkspitze (2471m) to the south. Both are easily accessible and I can recommend the latter for its views: easy path to a fine ridge, about 50mins there and back.

Although the Ignaz-Mattis Hut by the Unterer Giglach See now looks quite near, the route to it is roundabout: SE, then east to the

Znachsattel (2059m), then due north past the newish Giglachsee Hut (private), to the Preuneggsattel (1953m) and NE to the Ignaz-Mattis Hut (1986m). (1986)

(Before the description of the route from this hut to the Keinprecht Hut, here is the approach from the Enns Valley - also an escape route in the event of bad weather.)

2. IGNAZ-MATTIS HUT (1986m Cat. I) AND KEINPRECHT HUT (1872m Cat. I)

From Schladming drive or take a bus up the Obertal to the Hopfreisen Alm (1040m) at the junction of two valleys, the continuation of the Obertal to the left (SE) and the Giglachtal to the right (SW). Take the latter through forest at first and past a beautiful cascade on the Giglach Bach below the Lackner Alm. Up to the alm, then a steep climb (left) above the alm, followed by a traverse: across the hollow containing the alm there is an extraordinarily high and narrow waterfall. The Landauer See at 1654m can be seen far below.

The country now becomes more open with the broad pastures of the Giglach Alm, where beef-bulls wandering about can be intimidating, though theoretically harmless. There is a scattering of ruined huts, too, presumably from the days when there was mining in these mountains. Above the pastures we reach the Unterer Giglach See and on its west side, well placed to see and be seen, the Ignaz-Mattis Hut, built in 1910 and enlarged between 1965 and 1970. You may find quite a lot of day-visitors there, too, as it can be reached in only 1$^{1}/_{2}$ hours from the car park at the Ursprung Alm (1610m) at the head of the Preuneggtal.

Next day, return to the foot of the lake and fork right (SE). The ascent from here to the Rotmanndlscharte (2340m) is beautiful and interesting: red rocks, old mine-workings, the Dachstein to the north. Just beyond the Scharte the Rotmanndlspitze (2453m) lies directly on our route, and though it is 'insignificant' as a summit, it has wonderful views, especially NE, 800m down to the Duisitzsee (1648m) and to the Hochgolling in the east but, indeed, in every direction the scene is outstanding - north, the Dachstein; west, the Steirische Kalk Spitze (and a final glimpse of the Ignaz-Mattis Hut); south and south-west, the Sauberg and the Engelkarspitze.

Fairly steeply down on the east side, then easily over a rock-filled basin to the Krugeckscharte (2303m). The view of the Hochgolling from here has been used as cover-picture for the German *Kleiner Führer* to the area: need one say more? Soon you will see the Keinprecht Hut far below you, but *keep to the path*, due east. A memorial to a young man who lost his life over the cliffs when trying to take a short cut here is a grim warning! The long detour is unavoidable.

If you are going down there are two routes back to Hopfreisen from the Keinprecht Hut. The more direct, and better for ascent, goes NE, picturesquely, down to Neu Alm, continuing NNW to the Eschach Alm (1213m). There is parking here as well as at Hopfreisen. Less direct but grander is the high-level path that branches left (in descent) near the Neu Alm and traverses the eastern slopes of the Duisitzer Hahnkamp above the Obertal-Bach, to the photogenic Duisitzer See (we saw it from the Rotmanndlspitze) with its privately owned Duisitzsee Hut (1700m). It is steep from here to the Eschach Alm, and if your car is at Hopfreisen, or if you are catching the bus, you must finish along 4km of road.   (1976. Duisitzer See: 1972)

3. KEINPRECHT HUT (1872m. Cat. I) - LANDAWIRSEE HUT (1985m. Cat. I) - GOLLINGSCHARTE (2326m) - HOCHGOLLING (2863m) - GOLLING HUT (1683m)

Start as for the descent into the Obertal but soon fork right and pass a small building to traverse the head of the valley, later swinging NE in a great parabola. Then go east, climbing steeply, to the Trockenbrotscharte (Dry Bread Pass, 2237m). (The former path from Neualm to the Scharte is long disused and would be impossible to trace.)

You can now see the Landawirsee Hut some 250m below you. About one-third of the way down do not take the path on the left to the Gollingscharte marked *Nur für Geübte* even if you want to bypass this hut: in some conditions it can be dangerous.

The two Landawirseen (lakes) above the hut are worth a visit. The Hochgolling, the highest mountain in Styria, may be climbed from the Gollingscharte en route for the next hut or as a splendid rucksack-free expedition in its own right.

Leave the hut by the Mariapfarr jeep track, losing about 200m in height, then branch left. The path is grassy at first, then more scrambly to the left of a small gorge. Above this, notice the sign for the high-level approach: the potentially very dangerous section above an extremely deep snow-filled gully can be clearly seen. Finish up scree and (almost always) snow to the bleak and rocky Gollingscharte.

The Hochgolling

Start at a red-white-red waymark with an arrow '778 Golling'. This is the 'Historic' path, 1811, though an anonymous party had reached the summit by another route in 1791. Traverse right - metal stirrups on one exposed slab - and round on to the wild expanse of the west face up which the route rambles chiefly on scree.

(A sign to the left gives the way to the N.W. Grat, harder than the normal route. There are slabs, and a rope is needed. Grade II.)

Just after this you have a choice to reach a prominent 'stone man' on a small spur: the lower is easier but involves loss of height, the upper includes one or two tricky moves across slabs. Beyond the spur the route steepens. A former 'bad step' has iron stirrups set in the rock-face. The ridge is reached just north of the summit cross: superb views in every direction. Return to the Gollingscharte by the same route.

From the Gollingscharte keep off the snow and well to the right, avoiding a boulder field, then in steep, wide zig-zags down scree on the right of the corrie, leading to a crossing to the left and more zig-zags to the level, green floor of the Gollingwinkel: green because watered by underground streams. Pause to gaze up the awesome NE precipices of the Hochgolling, 1200m high, and forming what is locally claimed to be 'the greatest natural amphitheatre in the world' (but doesn't this ignore the Cirque de Gavarnie?). Walk easily past the former Obere Steinwederalm to the Golling Hut.

(1986)

4. GOLLING HUT (1683m) - KLAFFERKESSEL - PREINTALER HUT (1656m) - HANS-WÖDL HUT (1523m).

(All three huts belong to the Preintaler Club)
Drive or take a bus up the Untertal to the Weisse Wand Guest-house (1058m). Parking is beyond this. (Better to use the bus if you are planning to go all the way to the Hans-Wödl Hut; car, if you are

coming down from the Preintaler Hut.)

Walk more or less due south along the Steinriesental (the continuation of the Untertal). Much of the scenically most attractive way ascends so gradually as to feel almost level, and the Hochgolling ahead provides inspiration; only the last 200m of the 600m ascent are steep, and these are relieved by the beauty.

The walk from the Golling Hut over the Greifenberg (2618m) and through the Klafferkessel to the Preintaler Hut is the climax of the Niedere Tauern High-level route.

Start NE and climb steeply to the Greifenbergsattel (2449m) - but if you set off in good time you will be in cool shadow. At the Saddle the views become superb. As so often, the Dachstein can be seen in the north. The Hochgolling peeps over intervening mountains. To the east there is a wildly jagged ridge. The Saddle boasts a large and lovely tarn, and there is a startling view SE down to the Lungauer Klaffersee. To the north the view is blocked by the dull-looking mass of the Greifenberg, now to be easily ascended - and transformed! The northern side of the mountain is precipitous and directly below our feet is the Klafferkessel, that labyrinth of rock and water. All around us tower rugged mountains in seemingly endless number.

If the ascent of the Greifenberg is rather dull, the descent via the east ridge gives full compensation with exposed scrambling and good fixed ropes. You may linger amid the wonders of the Klafferkessel! (But when visibility is poor beware of getting lost!) This way is the easier way to enjoy it, as there is a fall of about 300m between the Obere Klafferscharte (2516m) just below the Greifenberg and the Untere Klafferscharte (2286m) near the Greifenstein (2397m) a rock tower standing sentry-like guarding the lower gate to this wonderland. In the Untere Klafferkessel you will see the memorial plaque to Hans Wödl, the explorer of the area.

It may seem a long way down from here to the Preintaler Hut (1656m) at the Waldhornalm. It is a welcoming place and was (probably still is) run by the Höflehner family, who in winter run a guest-house in Schladming.

For starting or finishing at this hut there is a path of exceptional interest and scenic beauty from the Weisse Wand. From the hut it runs charmingly through alm country to the Riesachsee (1338m) skirting it on the NNE. Just beyond it is the Obere Gföller Alm, where you can enjoy your drink and savour the wonderful scenery. Below here the path is steeper, with close-ups of the spectacular Riesach Waterfalls. If you parked a car above the Weisse Wand you will find it here.

To continue on the high-level way, take the Robert-Höfer-Steig, just across the valley from the Preintaler Hut and then almost due north, an easy ramble up to the Neualmscharte (2347m) - surprisingly dramatic and rocky, and the wind can whistle through it. Down the other side, still steadily north, past the Obersee to the Hüttensee, near which is the homely Hans-Wödl Hut (1523m), which was, and maybe still is, kept by two brothers: identical twins. Philip Tallantire considers this the finest hut in the area for situation and scenery.

(Early in the season or after new snow take the 781 past the Neualm and over the Fitzscharte (2201m). This *adds* about 3hrs to the route.)

From this hut a steep descent of 300m to the Bodensee (1149m) -no, not *the* Bodensee! - where Fink's 'Forellenhof' specialises, as its name implies, in serving trout.

There is a public motor-road to this and sometimes a mini-bus service. Otherwise you must walk something like 10km to catch a bus on the main road. If you do the walk the other way you can normally book a seat in advance on a morning mini-bus from Schladming.

If you have left a car at the Seekarhaus you can easily recover it using train and bus from Schladming.

(Several visits 1972 - 1986)

XXV: Gailtaler Alpen (Lienz Dolomites)
(AVE 56)

Boundaries of the Group: The Drau from the junction with the Gailbach to the junction with the Gail - the Gail - Kartischer Sattel - Gailbach to the junction with the Drau.

(Of this group we are concerned only with the western end, south of Lienz, known as the Lienzer Dolomiten - Lienz Dolomites.)

The whole group is named from its southern boundary; the Lienz Dolomites are exactly what their name implies. The obvious base of exploring them is Lienz (see XX).

The best known walk from Lienz in this group is the "Drei Törl Weg" (Three Passes Way). This was clearly and fully described by John Williams in the Newsletter No.118, Summer 1993, of the Austrian Alpine Club, UK Branch. The walk described here is shorter and less demanding, though it has a sting, or problem, in its tail!

KARLSBADER HUT (2260m) AND KERSCHBAUM-ALM-SCHUTZHAUS (1902m) (3 days). *Route:* Lienz/Tristacher See - Dolomiten Hut (1620m) - Karlsbader Hut (2260m) - Kerschbaumer Törl (2285m)

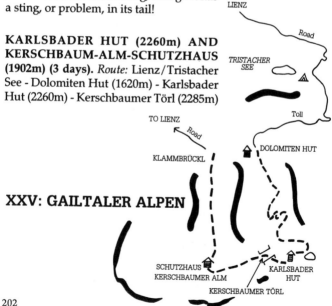

XXV: GAILTALER ALPEN

- Kerschbaum-Alm-Schutzhaus - Klammbrückl (1096m) - STING
IN TAIL
The free bus from Lienz to the Seewiese Campsite (see XX) continues
at certain times, though no longer free, up the toll road to the
Dolomiten Hut, privately-owned and dramatically perched on a
cliff-edge.

From here a good (private) road leads all the way to the
Karlsbader Hut. An older path, shorter, but steep and rough,
crosses the road from time to time and can be used to cut corners.

(A more difficult alternative, described by John Williams, is the Rudl-Eller-
Weg, involving steep ascents and fixed ropes.)

The scenery, even as appreciated by the road-walker, is
magnificent and the memorial Chapel at the Instein Alm (no actual
alm) is worth a few minutes' diversion. The Karlsbader Hut is large,
but often very full, and is beautifully situated by two lakes and
surrounded on three sides by dolomitic peaks and pinnacles.

From the hut, Route 213, known also as the Kärntner Grenzweg,
is a fine, traversing path that drops from the hut, SW, to keep below
precipices, swings a little NW, then climbs steeply up well
constructed zig-zags to the Kerschbaumer Törl (2285m).

The Karlsbader Hut, the routes to it and the jagged peaks
beyond it, form an impressive spectacle. But ahead, on the western
side of the Törl, the landscape is astonishingly different. You see
before you a huge and beautiful basin where pastures and woodlands
are surrounded by rocky mountains, steep, but less jagged than
those you are leaving behind: still a veritable Shangri La with no
vehicular way into it at all, though in 1995 an argument was going
on locally about a possible road.

You set off down quite steeply.

(An allegedly less steep, but much longer way goes sharp left from the Törl
to the Zochen Paß (2260m) and thence on the Zochsteig (215) to the hut.)

The hut can soon be seen, but it is one of those that seems to
retreat as you approach it, and even after you reach the valley floor
you have to bear round to avoid the steep head of the Kerschbaumer
Tal, and finally to cross a wide and stony riverbed. The hut, which
is owned by the Austrian Tourist Club (ÖTK) is simple without
crudity. Heating is by stoves, lighting by candles, and there is an
outside wash-place. The Wibmer family were running the hut in

1995 and Herr Wibmer was very friendly.

The descent route runs virtually parallel with that from the Dolomite Hut to the Karlsbader Hut. It is fantastically beautiful and very steep at first, especially near a typical limestone waterfall that pours down within a vast cleft. Some way below this the path ahead had fallen away (1995) and it was necessary to turn sharp right on to the (private) road. Further along a rather crudely-made notice from Herr Wibmer warned of the land-fall and closed path. Further along again you reach the Klammbrückl, a picturesque bridge over the deep Klamm or gorge through which rushes the Galizer Bach. Cars can park here, at the upper limit of the public road.

Here you encounter the sting in the tail of this three-day walk. You have the choice of four courses:

1. To return to the Dolomite Hut, essential if you drove up there instead of using the bus; but this involves a steep pull-up from 1096m to 1620m. Cross the bridge, take the path to the left (10A, the F. Lerch Weg), but leave it soon to turn right up path 12B.

2. Start on the F. Lerch Weg; don't turn off on 12B but continue down. The path becomes the Goggsteig. This is said to be very steep and was not recommended by Herr Wibmer. It leads to the Goggkreuz at Amlach, whence, if you are on the Seewiese Campsite, you can reach home on an almost level path (11A & 11) past the Tristacher See.)

3. Use the hard-top public road, the Stadtweg. It is long and wearying and swings further and further left in big zig-zags to avoid the Galitzerklamm, eventually crossing the Drau near a bus stop about 5km outside the town. (Bus timetable not known). This is what we did but were profoundly grateful when we were picked up on the zig-zags by the young Herr Wibmer in his Land-Rover-type vehicle, who took us right into the middle of Lienz!

4. Best of all perhaps: Herr Wibmer will gladly ring up for a taxi to meet you at the Klammbrückl. But you will need to estimate your time reasonably accurately. The official time, hut to bridge, is $1^{1/2}$hrs. We took 2hrs 45mins...but then we aren't as young as some of you!) (1995)

CICERONE GUIDES

Cicerone publish a wide range of reliable guides to walking and climbing worldwide

FRANCE, BELGIUM & LUXEMBOURG

THE BRITTANY COASTAL PATH - Castle

CHAMONIX MONT BLANC - A Walking Guide. Collins

THE CORSICAN HIGH LEVEL ROUTE: GR20 . Castle

FRENCH ROCK Birkett

THE PYRENEAN TRAIL: GR10. Castle

THE RLS (Stevenson) TRAIL. Castle

ROCK CLIMBS IN BELGIUM & LUXEMBOURG Craggs

ROCK CLIMBS IN THE VERDON Newcombe

TOUR OF MONT BLANC Harper

TOUR OF THE OISANS: GR54 Harper

TOUR OF THE QUEYRAS Castle

TOUR OF THE VANOISE Reynolds

WALKING IN THE ARDENNES Castle

WALKING THE FRENCH ALPS: GR5 Collins

WALKING IN HAUTE SAVOIE Norton

WALKING IN THE TARENTAISE &
BEAUFORTAIN ALPS
Akitt

WALKING THE FRENCH GORGES (Provence) Castle

WALKS IN VOLCANO COUNTRY (Auvergne) Castle

THE WAY OF ST JAMES: GR65 Bishop

FRANCE / SPAIN

WALKS AND CLIMBS IN THE PYRENEES Reynolds

ROCK CLIMBS IN THE PYRENEES Walker

SPAIN & PORTUGAL

WALKING IN THE ALGARVE Parker

ANDALUSIAN ROCK CLIMBS Craggs

BIRDWATCHING IN MALLORCA Stoba

COSTA BLANCA ROCK 1997 edition Craggs

MOUNTAIN WALKS ON THE COSTA BLANCA Stansfield

ROCK CLIMBS IN MAJORCA, IBIZA & TENERIFE Craggs

WALKING IN MALLORCA New Ed Parker

THE MOUNTAINS OF CENTRAL SPAIN Oglesby

THROUGH THE SPANISH PYRENEES: GR11 Lucia

WALKING IN THE SIERRA NEVADA Walmsley

WALKS & CLIMBS IN THE PICOS DE EUROPA Walker

THE WAY OF ST JAMES: SPAIN Raju

**SWITZERLAND including adjacent parts of France
and Italy**

THE ALPINE PASS ROUTE Reynolds

THE BERNESE ALPS Reynolds

CENTRAL SWITZERLAND Reynolds

CHAMONIX TO ZERMATT The Walker's Haute Route
Reynolds

THE GRAND TOUR OF MONTE ROSA (inc Italy) 2 vols
Wright

WALKS IN THE ENGADINE Reynolds

THE JURA - Walking the High Route and Winter Ski
Traverses Reynolds & Evans

WALKING IN TICINO Reynolds

THE VALAIS - A Walking Guide Reynolds

GERMANY / AUSTRIA / EASTERN EUROPE

WALKING IN THE BAVARIAN ALPS Bourne

GERMANY'S ROMANTIC ROAD A guide for walkers and
cyclists McLachlan

HUT-TO-HUT IN THE STUBAI ALPS Hartley

THE HIGH TATRAS Saunders & Renata

KING LUDWIG WAY Speakman

KLETTERSTEIG - Scrambles. Werner

MOUNTAIN WALKING IN AUSTRIA Davies

WALKING IN THE BLACK FOREST Speakman

WALKING IN THE HARZ MOUNTAINS Speakman

WALKING IN THE SALZKAMMERGUT Speakman

NORTHERN EUROPE

WALKING IN NORWAY Roos

*Ask for our catalogue which also shows our UK
range of guidebooks to walking - short walks,
family walks, long distance treks, scrambling,
ice-climbing, rock climbing, and other adventurous pursuits.*

*Other guides are constantly being added to the Cicerone List.
Available from bookshops, outdoor equipment shops or direct (send for price list)
from CICERONE, 2 POLICE SQUARE, MILNTHORPE, CUMBRIA, LA7 7PY*

CICERONE GUIDES

Cicerone publish a wide range of reliable guides to walking and climbing worldwide

ITALY & SLOVENIA

ALTA VIA - High Level Walks in the Dolomites. Collins

THE CENTRAL APENNINES OF ITALY Walks, scrambles & Climbs. Fox

THE GRAND TOUR OF MONTE ROSA (inc Switzerland) 2 Vols. Wright

WALKS IN ITALY'S GRAN PARADISO Price

LONG DISTANCE WALKS IN THE GRAN PARADISO Akitt

ITALIAN ROCK - Rock Climbs in Northern Italy. Churcher

VIA FERRATA - Scrambles in the Dolomites. Höffler/Werner

WALKING IN THE DOLOMITES Price

WALKS IN THE JULIAN ALPS Brown

MEDITERRANEAN COUNTRIES

THE ATLAS MOUNTAINS 2nd Edition. Smith

CRETE: Off the beaten track. Haughey

WALKING IN CYPRUS Brown

THE MOUNTAINS OF GREECE Salmon

THE MOUNTAINS OF TURKEY Smith

TREKS & CLIMBS IN WADI RUM, JORDAN Howard

THE ALA DAG - Climbs & Treks (Turkey) Tüzel

HIMALAYA

ANNAPURNA TREKKERS GUIDE Reynolds

EVEREST - A TREKKER'S GUIDE Reynolds

LANGTANG, GOSAINKUND & HELAMBU A Trekker's Guide. Reynolds

ADVENTURE TREKS IN NEPAL O'Connor

OTHER COUNTRIES

MOUNTAIN WALKING IN AFRICA 1: KENYA Else

OZ ROCK - A Rock Climber's guide to Australian Crags Lee

ROCK CLIMBS IN HONG KONG Heard

TREKKING IN THE CAUCAUSUS Kolomiets & Solovyev

ADVENTURE TREKS - WESTERN NORTH AMERICA Townsend

CLASSIC TRAMPS IN NEW ZEALAND Roos

GENERAL OUTDOOR BOOKS

THE ADVENTURE ALTERNATIVE Mortlock

ENCYCLOPAEDIA OF MOUNTAINEERING Unsworth

FAMILY CAMPING Bignell

FAR HORIZONS - Adventure Travel for All! Unsworth

THE TREKKER'S HANDBOOK Gilchrist

FIRST AID FOR HILLWALKERS Renouf & Hulse

THE HILLWALKERS MANUAL Birkett

LIMESTONE -100 BEST CLIMBS IN BRITAIN

MOUNTAIN WEATHER New Edition. Pedgley

SNOW & ICE TECHNIQUES Marsh

ROPE TECHNIQUES IN MOUNTAINEERING Marsh

CANOEING

CANOEIST'S GUIDE TO THE NORTH EAST Doll

SNOWDONIA WILD WATER, SEA & SURF Storry

WILDWATER CANOEING Barlow

CARTOON BOOKS IDEAL GIFTS

ON FOOT & FINGER Watson

ON MORE FEET & FINGERS Watson

LAUGHS ALONG THE PENNINE WAY Pete Bogg

THE WALKERS Watson

A full range of guidebooks to walking - short walks, family walks, long distance treks, scrambling, ice-climbing, rock climbing, and other adventurous pursuits worldwide

---

Other guides are constantly being added to the Cicerone List.
Available from bookshops, outdoor equipment shops or direct (send for price list)
from CICERONE, 2 POLICE SQUARE, MILNTHORPE, CUMBRIA, LA7 7PY